Never-Ending Prayer

Love, of course, has its own place in the framework of the autonomy discourse: it is a virtue that one cultivates, an expression of self in relation to others. In the context of the Christian tradition, however, another dimension of love comes to the fore: love as response, as the entering of a space that is opened up by others, as the appropriation of a story that others tell about the self. It is that dimension that is dominant in the perspective of guilt and reconciliation: love as a relation to which one entrusts oneself. That is the birthplace of the self – not in the sense that the self completes its identity by exercising the virtue of love, but in the sense that it is called into being by the love of others, and ultimately by the love of God.

Never-ending prayer experiences the triad self-God-world as a chain of love. That chain 'reveals' itself as the merciful encouragement to love God and neighbour. The proper opening statement of the self is not 'I think therefore I am', but *amor ergo sum* (I am loved, therefore I am).

5

God

The death of God has become a cliché, but it seems impossible to come to terms with it. Discussions about God are permanently frustrated by confusion of tongues and concepts. The 'scientific' conviction that the existence of a god is incompatible with contemporary knowledge collides with the 'naive' realism of the believer's testimony. The hypersensitivity of militant atheists is embarrassed by the apparent unconcern of traditional religious imagination in which 'God' remains unquestioned. Numerous compromises are in the making and have been made, but so far none of those is universally convincing. Postmodern theologians speak about God in a tongue-in-cheek manner: it is difficult to be faithful to a religious tradition and at the same time be credible to a wider audience.

It is obvious that the Christian tradition, if it wants to remain faithful to its traditional God-talk, needs to find new access to it as well as new arguments for its necessity. The death of God may not spell the end of the tradition as such, but it does imply a sensitive loss of accessibility of its contents. On the other hand, it brings to light that belief in God has never been a matter of course – not even in the days when the existence of a 'highest being' was generally accepted. In any case, the significance of the use of a God-image needs to be specified in some detail.

God is dead

The death of God is usually taken to mean that a (mono)theistic world view is no longer dominant in modern culture. More specifically: the age of the uneasy alliance between biblical God-talk and western philosophical reasoning about the 'highest being' is past. Of course, the death of God is closely related to the popularizing of scientific thinking that finds a natural ally in atheism. But it has more aspects. Of crucial importance is the suspicion that perceives forces of class struggle, passion and will to power behind belief in God, and explains religious faith as a pacifier for unstable people. That suspicion is accompanied (a second aspect) by a profound disenchantment about modernity as a tool for progress. The extreme violence of the twentieth century has undermined belief both in progress and in providence. A third aspect is the postmodern crumbling of traditions, along with the growing conviction that a consensus about truth is impossible. The recent comeback of religion shares in that crumbling. Rather than being a countermovement against the death of God, which it is sometimes taken to be, it confirms that death. God dies the death of thousands of individual religious constructions.

The problem we are dealing with is more fundamental than the disappearance of traditional forms of faith or the loss of support for church institutions. It is the inability to understand the world in the framework of a widely shared encompassing vision, and the absence of a transcending point of reference for life and society. It is the loss of religious imagination as a common cultural activity. Of course, on an individual level all these things remain important for numerous people. But those people face the challenge of 'reinventing' God without the support of a broad consensus.

The death of God means that it is no longer possible to appeal to something like a universally present notion of God that all human beings supposedly share, however tacit or unconscious it may be. It can no longer be presupposed that the word 'God' in public discourse is generally understandable. And when the cultural consensus about 'God' no longer exists, it has become impossible to use the same 'grammar' in discourse about God and in discourse about nature and history. In other words, the loss of cultural consensus deprives 'natural theology' – according to which the world as it is observed and experienced contains some reference to God – of its language.

Another thing to consider is that much contemporary Christian theology is no longer convinced that a 'theistic' concept of God (God as the omnipotent, omnipresent creator who 'rules' both nature and history) is a necessary part of the Christian faith. Theism is in fact a philosophical model, intended to enhance the compatibility of the Christian tradition with modern world views. One of its most serious shortcomings is that it cannot do justice to the great variety of existential experiences with faith, notably with the problem of evil. The fact that theism is no longer generally embraced suggests that Christian faith and atheism are more similar to each other than is often assumed.

Of course, there are fundamental differences between Christian faith and atheism. First of all, for atheism the death of God is a final conclusion, whereas for Christian faith it is a marking point that necessitates and encourages further reflection about God. Secondly, an aggressive atheism that considers faith in God as such to be harmful for humankind can, from a Christian point of view, only be opposed. An atheism that distrusts and suspects all religious imagination on the basis of a 'scientific' world view is short-sighted, as argued earlier. Nevertheless, there are forms of atheism that are in fact companions of never-ending prayer. There is an atheism that considers concrete images of gods as obstacles to true and complete reconciliation; and there is an atheism of permanent doubt that is afraid that concepts of God are in fact wishful but misleading fictions of stability. These forms of atheism can in fact contribute to deeper insight in the Christian tradition. More strongly: Christian God-talk that refuses to be challenged by them and arms itself against them may not yet have discovered the constructive role of doubt in the pilgrimage of faith.

After the death of God, the question whether or not God 'exists' can no longer be answered in an either/or way. Prayer assumes the reality of God's presence, but that does not necessarily imply the 'belief' that God somehow exists as a physical or anthropomorphous phenomenon in observable reality. Besides, 'belief' that something is or may be the case can refer to a position that does not necessarily involve personal commitment, such as is characteristic of prayer. It belongs to the nature of never-ending prayer that it cautiously winds it way past all these possibilities. The existence of God is neither a simple fact nor a simple non-fact. Never-ending prayer leaves both options of simplicity behind.

God is there

Prayer is not preoccupied with God as such. 'Seeing' or 'knowing' God is not its goal. What counts is God's presence in the cluster self-God-world. Prayer lives and moves in the faith that there is an 'eternal frame' in which self and world can relate to each other in a meaningful and hopeful way. In the language of the Christian tradition: God does not reveal himself but his 'being there'. God takes shape to the extent that prayer penetrates reality in its own unique way.

The ongoing effort of never-ending prayer to appropriate the perspective of reconciliation and to 'see' the world in that perspective brings God to the fore. God is not 'there' as a highest being that might also be loving and reconciling. It is the other way around: the shape of God is the personal condensation of the perspective of reconciliation to which prayer entrusts itself. One could also say: the 'existence' of God is not independently 'given'; it is essentially related to the experience of grace. This is not to say that the perspective of reconciliation precedes faith in God. The point is that God's 'being there' is connected to reconciliation from the start and that, conversely, the struggle of faith with the perspective of reconciliation comes to rest in the image of God who is love. The dynamic of the God-image is tied up with the dynamic of never-ending prayer.

That amounts to saying that religious imagination discovers and inscribes God in reality: God is there because and as soon as imagination gives expression to the conviction that the narrative of reconciliation is decisive. The presence of God is at the same time a product of imagination and a 'real given'. There is no relation of cause and effect here, only simultaneity. God's 'being there' is the discovery that reality is not merely inexhaustible and possibly threatening, but also definable along the lines of reconciliation. Reality is open in the sense that it is welcoming, and personal in the sense that it can be 'heard' as a narrative and an appeal.

We touch on a problem here that has been a serious puzzle for modern theology. It can be summarized in the question: projection or revelation? Is God the product of wishful thinking, of frustrations and desires that characterize the human psyche, or is God an independent actor who imparts knowledge to those who open themselves to him? That dilemma presents itself when the human mind and 'objectively' existing reality are treated as separate fields that need to be brought into contact. What is ignored, in that case, is that imagination and reality are inseparable parts of one dynamic: 'reality' is not reality by itself, but becomes reality through imagination. In that dynamic, furthermore, the self is more recipient than creator – in other words: the inseparability of imagination and reality has the structure of dialogue and response. One could also say: imagination always contains an element of revelation. That element is further articulated by religious imagination, in this case by the Christian narrative, in which 'revelation' is preferably associated with God. In this approach, 'projection or revelation' no longer constitutes an either/or dilemma. It can be very useful to investigate mechanisms of projection in the reflection on faith, but the mere fact that projection plays a role in faith does not necessarily rule out the possibility and the significance of revelation.

Against this background, there can be no objection against calling the ways in which God is inscribed in reality 'revelation' – on one condition. The concept of revelation is often used in connection with a view that localizes God in a 'supernatural' realm, from where he is supposed to communicate and reveal himself through special persons or events. Revelation of or from God is then seen as the final ground that justifies faith, scripture and tradition – final in the sense that it simply must be accepted. That approach is untenable. Its problem is the assumption that there are two 'worlds', a view that is incompatible with the insight that reality is one, albeit inexhaustible. The appearance of that one reality in imagination and reason is the framework in which also faith and God must be understood. Revelation is not a signal from some other reality, but it is the 'coming out' of the one reality as essentially related to God.

It may be objected that we are circumnavigating the question of God's existence by constructing a dialectical 'coincidence of opposites', namely 'God is dead' and 'God is there'. However, this is the only way in which some justice can be done to the difficulty that God-talk is both impossible (in terms of public rationality) and necessary (in terms of Christian religious imagination); and it is the only way to avoid an all-too-simple yes/no game. The distance between 'God is dead' and 'God is there' is bridged in the Christian narrative; more precisely: in never-ending prayer. That narrative and that prayer are not miraculous interventions from some 'outer space', but intertwined with the dynamic of human imagination as such.

God withdraws

We now introduce a second coincidence of opposites, namely 'God withdraws' versus 'God is near'. At first sight, this refers to the widespread experience of believers that God is alternately absent and present, but that is not what is meant here. The point is that the focus on reconciliation introduces a specific dynamic in the triad self-God-world. God intervenes in the relation between self and world; that intervention increases the distance between them in the sense that the world becomes larger, more complicated, more threatening because of its unreconciled character – and at the same time the intervention draws the self towards the world with a new intensity, precisely because of the focus on reconciliation. The interplay of God's withdrawal and his nearness has always figured prominently in the idiom of the Christian tradition, but it has not always been understood in this perspective.

We go back to what was said in the chapter on prayer about the unmistakability and the unknowability of God. In terms of the present chapter this means that the static concept of 'existence' in the case of God is replaced by the dynamic of God's simultaneous being and non-being, and by a movement of revealing and hiding. Christian God-talk has time and time again tried to steer a middle course between a comfortable atheism and an equally comfortable belief in a supreme being. A good example of such a middle course is negative theology. Negative theology claims that God is unknowable, that is to say that no statement can be valid that describes God as analogous with anything in observable reality. According to this claim, the statement that God does not exist does more justice to God than the statement that he does. To be sure, there is a great difference between negative theology and modern atheism. Negative theology does not consider faith in God to be impossible or absurd. To the contrary: denial of God is meant to respect God's deity and to make faith possible. Here, denial is an act of faith. In the perspective of negative theology, never-ending prayer is indeed never ending, in the sense that it never reaches its destination but keeps proclaiming its not-knowing. Prayer is even inclined to be suspicious when the God-image becomes too familiar. It realizes very well that an image of God is almost by implication also a trivialization of God – something that faith should avoid at all costs.

However, the withdrawal of God involves more than just the distance between the finite and the infinite, as negative theology suggests. More important is the distance between guilt and reconciliation. The faithful self learns to place itself in the perspective of guilt and reconciliation and thus to discover a God who is ultimate love. That perspective, however, includes not only the self as such but also the larger patterns of life and ultimately the whole world and all of humankind. The self becomes a participant in an encompassing guilt-and-reconciliation-history; it is taken along on a journey of ever-new discoveries of the guilt-condition of humankind, and of parallel discoveries of its own involvement in that condition. There is always more world and more humankind than can be imagined at any given moment. Never-ending prayer is stretched, lured as it were, beyond the preoccupation with what is at hand. That is what the withdrawal of God implies: it opens more world, more humankind, more future, not only in terms of quantity but especially in terms of quality. In other words: the perspective of guilt and reconciliation is like a magnifying glass. The self is brought face to face with the unreconciled character of the world: the widespread suffering, the pervasive mechanisms of exclusion and oppression, the violence-breeding inequalities. In the confession of guilt (which includes the world), the victims of that unreconciled character become visible. In this sense, the withdrawal of God into the infinity of the world contains a judgment: God becomes 'the other' who challenges the self to identify with 'the others'.

Without this withdrawing movement God is not 'complete', and neither is the self. We could describe it with the aid of the traditional concept of omnipresence – which would then mean, not that God 'is' everywhere, but that God is always ahead in his reconciling activity. 'Omni' in that case refers to future and to direction; it is a here-and-now that is at the same time a not-yet. The truth of negative theology is not that the finite cannot comprehend the infinite, but that the pressure of ultimate reconciliation calls forth an ever-widening gap. The presence of the withdrawing God is the embedding of existence in a sobering, puzzling but hopeful 'not-yet' of reality. 'Omnipresence' includes the ultimate ascendancy of fullness of being.

From here, a further step is in order. When we say that the withdrawal of God includes not only the self as such but also the larger patterns of life and ultimately the whole world and all of humankind, we need to be more specific about those larger patterns. The wider peripheries by which the self is encircled are also addressed by the guilt and reconciliation perspective, but indirectly. The self is encircled by, taken up into, the 'realities' of history and nature. It is determined by complex networks of historical connections and all kinds of ecosystems and interactions of matter and energy. How does reconciliation apply to those?

At this point the traditional concepts of redemption and creation come into view. Analogous to the perspective of guilt and reconciliation, history is set in the perspective of confusion and redemption, and nature is set in the perspective of chaos and creation. Redemption means that history is delivered from the doom of an everlasting mechanism of rise and fall; creation means that all things are subjected to the call to become part of a coherent celebration of life.

God is related to the peripheries in ways that reflect and foreshadow reconciliation, not in the sense of a succession of events, but in the sense of radiations from a centre. Reconciliation, redemption and creation are boundary concepts. They do not refer to events that have taken place or will take place within time-space reality. They qualify reality as seen through the eyes of faith; they formulate the direction for never-ending prayer.

God is near

For many Christian believers, the nearness of God is a precious experience of comfort, challenge, security or critical exchange. This experience can be one of a sudden enlightening breakthrough or one of a permanent reliable presence. It is one of the effects of religious imagination that God is inscribed in reality, and that, as a consequence, all kinds of stories, images and rituals bring God close to daily life. As a result, life can become transparent as a gift and a challenge. It can become the stage for a play in which one is invited to participate.

There are two ways in which the nearness of God can be understood. The first is that deep impressions or shocks caused by specific encounters or events evoke the experience of a relation with a transcending reality, which is then associated with 'God', because that is the available vocabulary with which one is familiar. Those experiences can be linked together to constitute a faith that can be truly meaningful and supportive, but they remain private in the sense that they cannot be communicated. The exchange of such experiences is not necessarily an exchange about God. Their highly personal nature makes them vulnerable to the objection of 'just' being strong emotions.

The second way to understand God's nearness is focusing on the existential appropriation of the narrative of reconciliation, redemption and creation. One becomes part of a 'history of salvation' that is cherished and kept alive in a community of believers. The tradition of this community is internalized in never-ending prayer and translated into small everyday occurrences. This second way is an experience of nearness that can be communicated, because it is explicitly related to a tradition and a community. It can also incorporate experiences of the first kind, by detecting 'glimpses' of reconciliation, redemption and creation in those experiences and by making them part of a larger story.

We must, however, take account of the fact that the experience of God's nearness is not always a comfort zone in which the self can come to rest. Fright and horror, serious illness, the feeling that one's life is completely thrown apart by some encounter or event, a natural disaster that destroys all security – those experiences are also very often associated with 'God'. Likewise, when the nearness of God is lived and understood in terms of never-ending prayer and the internalizing of the tradition, believers can sometimes become obsessed with a deep sense of unreconciledness, of being lost and rejected. In all those cases, the nearness of God is a threatening presence.

It is not easy to bring all this together into one perspective. In fact, we need to consider a third kind of nearness, one that can be regarded as the complement of the withdrawal of God, discussed in the previous paragraph. That is not the nearness of sudden appearance or continuous presence, but it is the nearness of address. It is a nearness that brings the world to the doorstep of the believing self and calls the self to move out of the preoccupation with itself. It does not replace or devalue the first two kinds but it accompanies them as a permanent sign of warning. It contains elements of challenge and judgment. It confronts the self with the world along the lines of guilt and reconciliation, of confusion and redemption, and of chaos and creation, and calls the self to structure its own life along the same lines. It is a nearness that makes the withdrawal of God tangible.

This way of phrasing brings to light that 'withdrawal' and 'nearness' are not opposites but need to be held together. The deepest meaning of the nearness of God is that the self is taken by the hand and led into a vision, in which God is not only the personal comforter but the one who 'has the whole world in his hands'. All the different ways in which the nearness of God can be experienced, shared and proclaimed come together in the movement of withdrawal, in which God opens the vision of the total scope of his relation to the world. Withdrawal is an eschatological notion, which means that it refers to the final salvation of the world, the 'famous last word' of the Christian narrative. In eschatological perspective, withdrawal and nearness define and complement each other; in their mutuality they constitute the God-image of the Christian faith. Eschatological language is necessary to 'complete' the God-image; conversely, as long as the Christian tradition needs eschatological language to express itself, that God-image is irreplaceable.

God is one

It has always been a central conviction of the Christian faith that God involves himself in the world and in humankind. Together with the fact that God is experienced in a large diversity of ways and that a multitude of stories, experiences and images with relation to 'God' have emerged through the centuries, this conviction causes the unity of God to be a problem. How can God be conceived as the Sovereign One who is unaffected by change, caprice and arbitrariness, and at the same time as drawn into the uneasy balances between self and world? For the Christian faith, both aspects are essential, but how can they be united?

The difficulty of this question highlights the importance that the Christian tradition attributes to the unity of God. God must be one in the sense that he remains faithful to himself, thus anchoring his faithfulness to humankind; and God must be one in the sense that he is the only one – there can be no competition with other gods. This last point does not mean that the Christian tradition has to prove that it is 'exclusively true' in distinction from other religious traditions. The point is that there is no place, no situation, no area of life where God's being and action are not valid. There is both comfort and challenge in the belief that God is one.

This is the background against which the monotheistic character of the Christian faith has to be considered. Historically speaking, Christian monotheism rests on an uneasy alliance between Jewish tradition (the 'Old Testament') and Greek philosophy. In the writings of ancient Israel JHWH manifests himself as 'the only one': the God who liberates, judges and summons to peace and justice. In Greek philosophy, the focus is on the principle of unity beyond all that is; here religious imagination is subordinated to rational abstraction. Despite its uneasiness, the alliance between these visions has determined the structure of western thinking about God for centuries.

Never-ending prayer, as described in the preceding chapters, is by nature monotheistic: it is directed towards a harmonious balance between self, God and world. As long as monotheism represents the dynamic of that prayer, the uneasiness of the alliance between its two sources does not constitute a major problem. It does, however, as soon as monotheism turns into a static world view that is used to organize society. In fact, monotheism has been employed to justify and legitimize hierarchical structures; as such it has created conflicts between religion and science or between 'higher' and 'lower' cultures. It is the temptation of monotheism to turn the unity of God into a principle of an all-inclusive system. It is of crucial importance for the Christian tradition to avoid that pitfall.

One way to do that – to preserve the significance of the concept of monotheism while avoiding its serious liabilities – has been 'radical monotheism'. Radical monotheism is a way of emphasizing that prayer is truly 'never ending'. There is no final concept or image that is comprehensive enough to bring the pilgrimage to a close. This is negative theology with a practical connotation: God must not become a tribal god or a mascot of a closed society. A tradition or a community that justifies its closedness with an appeal to God amounts to 'little faith'; it gives up faith in God who is truly one. In radical monotheism, the faith that God is one becomes a constant reference to 'God beyond God'. During the pilgrimage of faith, God remains fragmentary, and at the same time it is the unity of God that keeps the pilgrimage going.

A second way to avoid the negative effects of monotheism has been trinitarian thinking: the early church doctrine that God 'is' in three modes of being that together express his unity. God the Father, God the Son, and God the Holy Spirit are three distinct 'presences' of God, but in all three it is the one God who presents himself. This way of thinking has given rise to much speculation, but it has been very significant for the self-understanding of the Christian tradition. Its *raison d'être* was (and is) the integration of a biblical concept of a God who is actively and lovingly engaged in the world and in humankind, into Greek modes of thinking that are primarily interested in an abstract 'principle of being'. If one wants to do justice to God's involvement in humankind and express that in the context of Greek thinking, it is inevitable to posit some 'divine activity' in the being of God himself. The tradition speaks here of the generation of the Son and the sending of the Spirit: these are considered to be movements both in history and in God. In this perspective, the unity of God is no longer the highest principle of being that is placed above all reality; rather, the unity manifests itself in the ongoing interaction between Father, Son and Spirit.

Trinitarian thinking is anti-monotheistic because it understands the unity of God along three lines simultaneously. In this chapter these are reconciliation, redemption and creation (traditionally: the Son, the Spirit and the Father). Also: the three movements 'God is there', 'God withdraws' and 'God is near' can be understood as references to respectively the Son, the Father and the Spirit. The issue in all this is not doctrinal correctness, but loyalty to a tradition that has always presented God as revealing himself in different ways. God is 'the Spirit who prays in us', who keeps the never-ending prayer going; God is 'the Son, the Word', who lays out and blesses the journey of humankind between guilt and reconciliation; God is 'the Father', the all-encompassing, eternally reliable partner-in-dialogue, and the actively forthcoming answer to prayer.

6

World

World is the summary of everything that matters. It includes and it confronts the self. It is the impersonal interaction of energy, matter, life and history in which the self lives, moves and has its being, but at the same time it challenges the self from outside. It is 'my' world in the sense that it is my particular excerpt of reality, but it is simultaneously the archetype of 'the other'. World is home but also threateningly foreign. It is both cradle and grave.

This introduction indicates how difficult it is to understand the meaning of 'world' in the triad self-God-world. The world as sketched in the preceding sentences implies God, but because self and world are at odds with each other God is usually imagined as occupying a 'third' position. 'God' and 'world' are both ultimate concerns for the self, sometimes separately, sometimes closely linked. In any case, the world is not just the scenery or the background of an independently advancing self-God relation, nor is the self just the spectator of an independent God-world relation. It is as part of a complicated three-ness that the world has its place in never-ending prayer.

Theistic imagination

It can be no surprise that the many diverse and often contradictory experiences of humankind with 'the world' have always been a fertile breeding ground for religious imagination. Nor can it be surprising that images of the world as an organized and stable 'cosmos' have always been attractive and popular and still abound in spite of all scientific advance.

According to those images, everything has its place in a divine design: life may be insecure but it is securely anchored in the encompassing structure of all things. Traces of this premodern wordview can still be found in the way in which everyday speech, earth-centred as it is, deals with celestial bodies and with the weather. But they can also be found in a view of God and world that is called 'theistic'.

Theism as such is not premodern, but it does try to secure elements of premodern thinking in confrontation with the challenges of modernity. It is modern in its tendency to see reality as a system that is governed by laws of cause and effect, of which God is the manager. It is premodern in its insistence that God controls everything, intervenes at will and maintains a personal relation with every single life. One problem with that image is that the 'supervising' function of God is posited prior to his reconciling, redeeming and creating action, making these actions appear to be secondary. The notion that God designs the universe is not easily combined with the assurance that God cares for every human being: many theological and religious problems originate from the notions of providence and predestination. Moreover, the idea that the whole cosmos is a divine work of art is in contrast with experiences of a world 'in the grip of evil'.

A second problem with theism is that it objectifies the 'world' as a coherent totality, which presupposes a God's-eye view that is simply not accessible to human experience. In human experience, the world – as part of the triad self-God-world – presents itself in different forms and on different levels. World is the permanent context of everyday life, and as such challenging and threatening, peaceful and unpredictable. But it is also history, a process in which large units of humankind successively constitute an arena of influence and conflict. And it is a system of life, an ecological universe and a theatre of evolution. Finally, it is an ever-expanding network of energy and matter. All those manifestations of 'world' simply cannot be brought together in a totality that is as such the object of human experience or of divine management.

(The same is true with regard to the massive concept of 'evil'. It makes a great deal of difference whether one speaks of life-threatening evil in a war, or of biological evil caused by viruses and microbes, or of 'physical' evil such as earthquakes and floods. There is little reason to bring all these evils together in one concept, unless one uses the common denominator 'everything that threatens human well-being'. The tendency to personify evil as a mythical power is, of course, a premodern phenomenon, but it can also function in theistic imagination: the Great Manager is confronted by the Great Disturber.)

The most serious problem with theistic imagination is, however, the role of science. Scientific inquiry has demythologized the world, not in the sense that there is no room left for imagination, but in the sense that imagination no longer has the power of explanation. Science has introduced a way of observing the world that excludes a transcendent reality. Historically speaking, there is no overarching plan, no destiny of humankind. Biologically speaking, there is no design that provides evolution with a goal and a direction. Physically speaking, there is no outer border to the universe. This way of observing has become generally accepted, and it no longer tolerates any theistic scheme, even though there are large numbers of people who hold on to such a scheme in an (uneasy) effort to keep faith and knowledge together.

It might be objected, that scientific language and imagination can very well coexist as complementary, as was in fact argued in the chapter on imagination. That is true: there is a great deal of biblical and religious imagination about God who is playing with the powers of nature and rescuing creatures from all kinds of distress. Such imagination visualizes important aspects of the Christian faith, and is not necessarily incompatible with a scientific world view. We do have a problem, however, when theistic imagination solidifies to become an alternative science that intends to compete with a 'pure' scientific approach – pure in the sense that it tries to steer clear of imagination. This 'competition' has caused too much confusion in modern times. The problem is not that there cannot be any discussion between diverging (scientific) theories, but rather that the expressiveness of religious imagination is severely hampered when all imagination about God the Creator is pressed into the straitjacket of a pseudoscientific discussion.

It is precisely with respect to 'world' that the relation between science, imagination and religion appears to be in disarray. Theistic imagination has been employed to compensate the loss of comfort that was the consequence of the loss of credibility of premodern thought, but it has caused (and still causes) confusion. It is gradually being replaced by a search for possible new points of contact between the Christian tradition and the modern world view. What does 'creation' mean when it is not alternative physics? How can the relation between God and world be imagined when we drop the images of maker and manager? How can biodiversity be related to the belief that God is concerned with life and death of each mortal? What is the kingdom of God in our present-day experience of history? The traditional images about God and world have not necessarily become useless; to the contrary, the eloquence of those images can be rediscovered again and again. But if they are not rediscovered in their powerful function as images, and if they are no longer connected with the experience that contemporary people have with 'world', tradition is in danger of losing its persuasiveness.

World as history

As discussed in the chapter on tradition, the construction of a 'time of one's own' is necessary for human identity. Directing one's own time implies the cherishing of memories and the visualizing of future; in other words: the construction of a private narrative. Without such a narrative there is no self. That narrative is part of general, 'objective' history and yet it is not. History consists of individual constructions and yet it is also experienced as an independent reality that precedes and includes those constructions. The self always finds itself caught up in a history that is already there. The course of that history determines the self like an impersonal 'wheel of fortune'.

Because of that experience, humankind has always been involved in efforts to explain and predict historical events. History has been presented as divided into successive 'ages' – ages that are supposed either to lead to a final end or to keep returning in an eternal cycle. Rituals of invocation and prediction, myths that provide human existence with a divine origin, prophesies that clarify the past in the light of divine wisdom, love and judgment and interpret the future as a divine promise – all those practices have expressed and still express the universal human desire to be redeemed from fate. Apocalyptic thinking anticipates the end of history as a *denouement*: justice will be done to the oppressed, oppressors will be punished.

To some extent, the Christian prayer for the coming of the kingdom of God voices the same desire to come to grips with the unpredictability of history. The kingdom of God is expected not only to 'end' history and to inaugurate radical renewal, but also to make sense of history as such. Often, the coming of the kingdom is associated with a final judgment in which humankind and history 'as a whole' are called to account.

Modern secularized approaches to history have long retained traces of such religious-mythological imagination, even though explicit references to the kingdom of God or a last judgment are no longer in vogue. For example, the idea that an all-including 'spirit' will manifest itself through the course of history, and the idea that history is 'moved' by a never-ending dynamic of revolution, have been widely popular. Much modern thinking has assumed that history as a whole can be planned around a design or a central conviction. More recently, the victory of 'human rights' or of 'capitalism' has been hailed as the 'end' of history.

It seems, however, that the last traces of such imagination are disappearing. Efforts to present the totality of history as an ongoing narrative with a beginning and an end are losing their credibility. What remains is an experience of history as an arena of collusions: between empires, nations, ideologies, civilisations, or major economic power blocks. If there is an overarching image at all, it is one of resentment, of permanent resistance on the part of those areas of humankind that have lagged behind the mainstream of power and prosperity. What remains, in other words, is an open question: is history the never-ending story of fundamental conflict, the everlasting rehearsal of unreconciledness, or is there some prospect of redemption? When references to a divine guidance, a divine promise, or a magic event that transforms everything have lost their point of contact with contemporary experience, how can redemption be imagined?

We remind ourselves again of the fundamental dynamic of memory and anticipation by which history is generated. Not only personal narratives, but also collective narratives of communities, nations and cultures are formed by that dynamic. When we confront history 'as a whole', we may experience an opaque totality of things beyond our control, but in fact we are incorporated into an infinitely expanding network of narratives. The expansion and multiplication of those narratives is not in itself problematic. What is problematic is that they have assumed the character of an ongoing battle that is both unstructured and destructive. That makes the unpredictability of history threatening, and it causes history to be experienced as an impersonal stream of things that overrules all individual effort to maintain a meaningful outlook. But that impersonal stream of things is in fact an arena of colliding systems of imagination. And that is not a 'wheel of fortune'; it is unreconciled humankind.

Against this background, redemption from the doom of ongoing historical events means breaking the logic of history in as far as that logic consists of a repetition of the battle of the many histories. It means a liberation from the ever-recurring tendency to create individual histories and futures separate from those of others. It is the overcoming of the 'hell of the others'. Redemption, understood in this way, is an implication and an extension of reconciliation. It is the anticipated future of a dynamic that begins 'simply' with the sharing of individual narratives and the reconciliation of memories.

Such reconciliation of memories is a never-ending process that pursues frictions and conflicts between individuals, communities, nations and cultures back into an ever-receding past. It is a process by which individual selves learn to appropriate the history to which they belong and from which they emerge. It is never-ending in the sense that it can never be complete. But it refers to a unity of humankind that includes a unity of histories.

The relation of 'God' and 'world' on the level of history, as conceived in never-ending prayer, is a redeeming relation: it is aimed at restoring humankind as a historical unity, at liberating humankind from the dynamic of separation, hostility and oppression. It is aimed at the unity of a humankind that creates time, tradition and identity. That is the 'kingdom of God'. The kingdom is not an external plan that hovers over history and is suddenly made to happen. It is not hidden in history as a self-realizing force of peace and justice. Rather, it is operative in history as a dynamic of guilt and reconciliation and as a promise of redemption. As such it is the antidote against all experiences of tragedy and meaninglessness that are so often linked to history.

World as evolution

The most influential confrontation between premodern religious imagination and science takes place in the field of biology. Many believers experienced the advent of evolution theory as a head-on attack on faith in God as creator, and even today many refuse to exchange the image of a personal and omnipotent creator for concepts such as selection and adaptation. Most religions cherish the mystery of life and the endless diversity in which it presents itself as a precious example of divine presence. Evolution theory was an unwelcome disenchantment, that not only challenged the uniqueness of every living being, but also the existence of divine design and the purposefulness of life as such.

The confrontation is not necessarily irreconcilable, except perhaps in the case of so-called creationism: a theory that claims to be an alternative biological science and considers evolution as an error. There are several efforts to establish some kind of agreement or even synthesis between 'evolution' and 'creation'. Yet, those efforts too have often been inclined to ignore the difference between religious imagination and explanatory theory and have tried to stage some form of competition. Such competition has been aggravated by defenders of evolution who were inclined to treat their theory as an infallible truth that proves the untenability of theistic thinking. It is of great importance for both sides to free the discussion from those constraints.

Generally speaking, evolution theory itself is no longer a pseudodoctrinal narrative. It is anti-doctrinal in the sense that it excludes all hints of design or purpose, and in doing so it rejects all premodern (including religious) imaginations about life in as far as these figure as alternative biological theories. Biologically speaking, there can be no external control, and neither can it be maintained that there is an inherent destination in all living things. But it does make a difference whether one follows the reductionist approach of neo-Darwinism (the *gen'* is the basic unit and all organisms are temporary vehicles of a permanent battle of selection), or more holistic theories, according to which complex systems of life are themselves units of selection and adaptation. In other words, the discussions about evolution do reveal the search for a *logos*, a coherence in the vast area of evolution-phenomena.

There is, for example, the discussion about organism and function. Is function – in other words, productive interaction between organism and context – something that just emerges, or does it follow from a preceding genetic constellation? Is adaptation 'blind', or does it create new coherences of meaning? Does evolution presuppose an ideal world of perfect adaptations, or is it just an ongoing dance of elements with a totally unpredictable outcome? Another example is the question of the identity of complex organic systems such as humans or animals. Identity is a more-or-less stable centre within ongoing movements of living and dying. The human body is both such a centre and such a movement (of living and dying cells). Do we have to speak of different identities on different levels within one organic system?

These and similar questions are passable roads for a religious imagination that is no longer preoccupied with issues of cause, origin and design. That preoccupation severely limited the possibilities of religious imagination about evolution, and it still does. There must be other ways to reflect on a meaningful self-God-world relation in the context of life on earth. A good starting point would be the awareness that all life on earth is intricately but unmistakably connected and interdependent. That is an important lesson about 'creation' that can be learned from evolution; it is confirmed by the manifold experiences of disturbance and imbalance since the advent of the 'anthropocene' age. This lesson highlights important aspects of the relation between humankind and nature. One of them is that human life is a struggle for survival, a serious battle among numerous other forms of life, with an uncertain outcome; another aspect is that the brief spans of individual human life are all part of ongoing age-long processes.

Additional complications come into view when the paradigm of evolution is not restricted to biological organisms but is extended to include social realities as well. An anthill is the classical example: it is a biological coherence of numerous independent organisms. Is that image applicable to human society? More strongly: is the earth itself comparable to a large-scale anthill? For some environmental scientists that is indeed a useful starting point. It would imply not only that humankind is only one part of an encompassing ecosystem, but also that the development of human societies can be understood as an evolutionary process of selection and adaptation.

The Christian tradition is full of images of creation and design, but when these are understood to imply that every single detail of life is subject to a preconceived plan, these images are difficult to combine with the lessons of evolution. Perhaps we should not think of a preconceived plan, but of a call to order. 'Order' – not understood as a static pattern in which everything has a fixed place, but as a successful arrangement of life. Life on earth, engaged as it is in an ongoing struggle for survival, is imagined as being beckoned in the direction of interdependence and fulfilment rather than chaos or destruction. Order in that sense is an extension of reconciliation and redemption. It is the outer circle of a dynamic of completion. In one word: it is creation.

Creation means the vision of peace between humankind and nature as the final prospect of an age-old war that has damaged both very severely. Analogous to the dynamics of reconciliation and redemption, creation refers to a road that seems to be practically impossible to travel, but above all to a final perspective for the dynamic self-God-world. Rather than to a specific divine action at the beginning of time and space, creation refers to a destiny of renewal that conceives of human relations and history as embedded in an immense theatre of life. Creation is an invitation to a dance.

World as cosmos

Scientific inquiry into the behaviour of the smallest particles and the largest stellar systems has practically destroyed all images of 'world' that humankind might have cherished in the past. The theories of relativity and quantum physics have created a seemingly unbridgeable distance between everyday life and scientific truth. Other than the domains of history and evolution, the cosmic reality does not appear to touch people's lives very deeply. But this may be an optical illusion. For it is precisely physics, even more than history and biology, that has gradually dismantled the premodern God-world image in the course of the last five centuries. This dismantling has become more abstract in recent years, but that only confirms the estrangement that was already in process.

Physicists are not interested in images of 'world', but in explanatory theories about energy and matter. Many of them have the ambition to develop a 'theory of everything'. Such a theory – the holy grail of science – would probably express in mathematical formulae what can be understood about nature at its most fundamental level. But it would not address the question as to whether there is such a thing as an 'objective reality' behind those formulae, let alone the question about a possible divine activity. If physics would address those questions, it would contradict its own self-definition. In modern physics the universe has no outer border.

That by itself is enough to cause estrangement between traditional religious imagination and a contemporary view of the cosmos. But there is more. For example: the position of the observer turns out to make a difference for what is observed: inquiry 'changes' reality. More strongly: according to some physicists, the most fundamental materials of nature are not minimal pieces of 'matter', but bits of information that cause links of energy and matter to happen. Another example is the basic uncertainty in nature that is revealed in quantum mechanics. In other words: there is not one objective reality behind different measurements. That is difficult to combine with the image of a creator who 'forms' heaven and earth in the same way in which an artist creates a piece of art, and of a creation that presents itself as an impressive painting in front of spectators. It is understandable that those images are pushed to the margin by an increasingly modern experience of 'world'.

In the search for new points of contact between religious imagination and a modern experience of 'world', attention has been drawn to the so-called 'big bang': a hypothetical explosion thirteen billion years ago that enabled rudimentary forms of energy and matter to form links that helped the universe on its way. Is that not similar to the religious conception of a creation out of nothing? A second example is the so-called 'anthropic principle': the curious fact that the human capacity to observe things is in harmony with the patterns of regularity in the universe. Does that not remind us of the central position that the human being has in the religious conception of creation? A third example:

the eleven dimensions that figure in string theory make it possible to imagine not only parallel worlds but also a kind of 'afterlife' in which human consciousness might exist under as-yet-unknown conditions.

For physics, however, those points of contact are not helpful. Physicists constantly warn against religious misuse of the fact that their theories sometimes border on speculation. The loose ends of physics should not be treated as bridges to faith in God or in supernatural interventions, and religious imagination should not make itself dependent on those loose ends. To be sure: questions about the origin of everything, about the position of the human being in the whole of reality and about the many dimensions are also religious questions that occupy people on an existential level. It is understandable, therefore, and to a certain extent also inevitable that the search for points of contact continues. In the observation of the cosmos, physics and religious imagination constantly encounter each other. Both play a role in the construction of narratives about origin and future of the world and of humankind. They do not leave each other alone. That in itself is a point of contact.

The heart of the matter is that never-ending prayer differs from science. Prayer does not start with the origin of matter, but with the 'discovery' of the loving concern of God. God made a start by calling his creatures forward together with and in the midst of nature. 'Things' form the visible, tangible and knowable 'stuff' of the call of God. Seen this way the world emerges in the context of prayer as 'creation'. The question about the origin of the relation of God with his creatures is not the question about the first manifestation of energy and matter. The praying self looks back on its own not-yet, and in that perspective also on the not-yet of the world. That faith-retrospective is part of the self-God-world dynamic in which the self comes to itself. Of course, that retrospective is accompanied by scientific questions about the origin of the cosmos, but the two do not coincide. There is a certain affinity between them, they attract and repel each other, they can neither be united nor separated, but in the end the difference remains. They cannot help each other in their respective searches; the suggestion that they can is a misunderstanding of both faith and science.

World as creation

Designating the world as 'creation' means affirming that it is permeated by divine creativity – a creativity aimed at a successful arrangement of life. It means that the numerous ways in which self and world are related are transformed into invitations to settle and to flourish. Creation is God's loving call to come forward and to overcome the lostness of a self that is lost in confusing relations with others, that is a victim of unpredictable events, complex patterns of evolution and abstract laws of physics. Creation means that the world is being arranged as a place where that call can be heard and answered.

Understanding the God-world relation in terms of creation is an implication of the perspectives of guilt and reconciliation and of redemption. It is the 'outer circle' of the triad self-God-world. It is not the religious adoration of the impressive construction of the universe or of the overpowering beauty of nature, and neither is it the passive resignation to an inscrutable divine guidance. To equate creation with nature leads to a serious confusion of tongues, for instance when respecting the 'integrity of creation' begins to mean a romantic mystification of evolution. That the world is creation is not an established fact; it is the constant embedding of contingent reality in divine attention. It is a qualification that needs to be discovered, heard, believed and lived through prayer.

The relation between creation, reconciliation and redemption can be phrased in yet another, slightly different way: creation and redemption are two 'divine movements' that are implied in the track of reconciliation. All humankind and all things are called into a coherence of salvation. Here it is important to hold creation and redemption together. Without creation, redemption becomes an escape from material reality into higher spheres of 'communion with God'. Conversely, without redemption, creation is the permanent repetition of a first movement instead of a completed work. Redemption is the ultimate expression of divine creativity, the implied aim of creation.

A faith that includes creation is an antidote to anthropocentrism. To say that creation is the 'outer circle' of the triad self-God-world is not meant to imply that the self is the centre. The centre is the divine dynamic of reconciliation and redemption that 'flares out' to include all things. It belongs to that dynamic that the self is called away from its self-centredness and is placed 'in the garden'. It is called to make itself part of creation and give up the illusion of a closed and self-sufficient self. On the other hand, a consistent response to that call makes clear that human beings are not just accidental phenomena in a vast impersonal universe, but *dramatis personae* in a theatre of salvation.

Creation means that all things are geared to communication, interaction and cultivation. It is a permanent movement from infinity to limitation, from immenseness to restriction, from universality to human concreteness. Creation is not preconceived design but contingency of love. In that sense it is linked to finitude, to the immediate context, rather than to cosmic dimensions.

Only along these lines can creation also be seen as the victory over evil. 'Evil' and 'creation' are not mythical powers engaged in an everlasting battle. Evil is the undeniable and inevitable shadow on all three levels of the human experience of world: history, evolution and cosmos. A self-God-world relation that understands itself in the perspective of God's loving invitation implies a permanent rebellion against evil. A negative answer to the question as to whether evil belongs to the 'good creation' is not a theoretical affair; it is not the outcome of speculation. Rather, it is a core element of never-ending prayer. The faith that evil does not belong to creation is like a wager. Prayer places all experiences of evil in the perspective of reconciliation, redemption and creation, and it does so 'without end'.

Review and Preview 2

Never-ending prayer, as described in the introduction to this book, is 'a sustained dynamic of questioning and searching, of preoccupation with the coherence of all things, of finding answers, of living in commitment. Prayer, thus understood, is truly "never ending": large as life itself. It is a never-ending triadic conversation between self, God and world, in which life in its fullness is sought, found, lost and found again. Images of faith and theological concepts live and move in the context of that conversation'.

Our case for the Christian tradition as never-ending prayer began with a focus on the double embeddedness of that tradition: the way in which it is intertwined with the fundamental human activity of imagination on the one hand and with the pilgrimage of humankind on the other. Special attention was given to the dialogical nature of human existence and the triadic structure of the self's being in the world. On the basis of that exploration, the chapters on self, God and world proceeded to sketch the content of the Christian faith – not as a confessional formula or a summary of doctrine, but as a two-way traffic: the experience of being-in-the-world 'meets' the tradition, and that encounter produces insights of faith. *Fides qua* and *fides quae* (the personal involvement and the formulated insights) are in constant interaction.

In the course of and as a result of that encounter, the self comes into view as taken up into the dynamic of guilt and reconciliation, and as called forward by divine love; God comes into view as the One who reconciles, redeems and creates; and the world comes into view as creation, destined to become a 'theatre of salvation'. Through all that, the self's being in the world is broadened and intensified; the self becomes a character in a world-encompassing narrative.

That encompassing narrative has an unmistakably eschatological character. The 'withdrawal' of God, as suggested before, means that God's reconciling, redemptive and creative action is being extended to include the whole world and all of history; in that sense it is always 'ahead' of any given configuration of self, God and world. The *eschaton* (the end) does not so much refer to future events; it is more like a vanishing point that puts all that is into perspective. It stretches the imagination again and again beyond all temporary experience, in the never-ending movement of prayer. To understand God in this way implies that 'self' and 'world' are given back to themselves, as it were; they are 'returned' from the *eschaton* to the present. The self receives itself in *eschatonomy*, as called forward by divine love; the world and human history are mobilized by the dynamics of creation and redemption.

There is a certain logic in the order in which self, God and world are reviewed: the self has a problematic relation with 'the other' and is confronted with the vision of reconciliation; God as the ultimate reconciler is omnipresent; and so the world comes into view as being reconciled, redeemed and created. This logic, however, does not imply that Christian faith necessarily begins with personal experiences of guilt and reconciliation. It can also be sparked by the way in which the tradition describes God in his triune activity or by specific impressions of 'world'. Sooner or later, the three points of reference in the triad will turn out to be interwoven.

The encounter between Christian tradition and being-in-the-world can take place in a large variety of situations. It can be sparked or intensified, for example, in situations of oppression and slavery; here, the prospect of liberation can become the key to a vision of history as judgment and redemption. Another example is the concern for the problems of nature: severe disturbances of ecological balance or the threat of climate change can become the occasion for a preoccupation with creation. Likewise, a concentration on the global refugee problem can lead to deeper reflection on the dialectic of human community (defensive and open) and on the vision of the unity of humankind. The war of identities (racism, feminism) brings the complications of a 'reconciliation of memories' to the fore. Winding its way through all those situations, the Christian tradition is enriched, changed, sometimes caricatured – but such is its history.

The weakness of the Christian tradition is that after the death of God its narrative is no longer welcomed by a broad cultural consensus. In the eyes of many it has become irrelevant and other-worldly, foreign to the preoccupations of secular humankind. The power that is hidden in this weakness lies in its stubborn focus on the largest possible coherence in which self, God and world can be imagined. That coherence is always larger than the provisional frames that are employed by religious individuals in their pilgrimage. Those provisional frames are sometimes construed by a prematurely satisfied need for stability; most often they reflect the human inclination to make the self-God-world problems smaller and more manageable than they are. Over against this inclination, never-ending prayer reflects the persistence of imagining reconciliation, redemption and creation in their true universal dimensions.

In its eschatological ambition, the Christian tradition positions itself among the many systems of religious imagination not primarily as a contestant for religious truth, but as a constant interference that focuses on intensifying and radicalizing the self-God-world triad. Its distinct characteristics are not specific conceptions of God, moral commandments or visions of life after death, let alone certain culture-related institutional expressions. Its message raises fundamental questions about the self in relation to guilt and reconciliation, God after the death of God, and the world in its dependence on redemption and creation. In that sense, it challenges all institutional expressions of religion, including those of the Christian tradition itself.

In this perspective, an additional comment is in order about the double embeddedness of the Christian tradition that was emphasized before. In spite of that embeddedness, the Christian tradition unmistakably maintains a certain inner distance toward the human pilgrimage as a whole, even while being part and parcel of that pilgrimage. The narrative of Christian faith flows into the general narrative of humankind while at the same time rewriting it. It offers a specific 'system of religious imagination', and at the same time it seeks to intensify and radicalize the self-God-world experiences in which all of humankind is involved. That is its mission. For the Christian faith, the unity of humankind is not an abstract combination of all possible systems of imagination; it can only be produced through reconciliation, redemption and creation.

So far, we have looked at the Christian tradition as a never-ending prayer orienting itself on the Christian 'reading' of the triad self-God-world. In this perspective, tradition is like a garden in which one walks around or a home in which one lives; tradition is the ecosystem in which one flourishes. With that, our 'case for the Christian tradition' has taken a significant step, but it remains incomplete. What is lacking is a second perspective, which highlights the fact that the Christian 'system of imagination' is a historical phenomenon construed by memory and anticipation. This system was shaped by specific historical events and it reshapes itself in specific historical communities. In this perspective, the pivotal point in the Christian tradition is the commemoration of Jesus Christ. The two perspectives support each other and refer to each other.

Together, they make clear that the Christian way of speaking about self, God and world is not 'simply there', but originates in a specific history. Conversely, commemorating and anticipating Jesus Christ is not an afterthought, not an added activity in the Christian tradition, but its very *raison d'être*. That will be the focus of the following three chapters.

7

Memory

The internal mechanism of memory and anticipation of the Christian tradition circles around Jesus Christ. The Christ-event is the driving force of never-ending prayer and the consistent point of reference in the triadic conversation of self, God and world. The Christ-event is present as *tradition*, which means that it is kept alive and continually recreated in the activity of remembering and anticipating communities. That looks relatively simple, but it is not without its complications. That the event is present as tradition inevitably implies that it is mediated by the experience and reflection of numerous generations of Christians. It is made present but hidden from view by thick layers of interpretation.

That problem presents itself to every new generation of believers. Faith seeks direct access to the Christ-event, it wants to come 'face to face with Jesus', but it is instead invited to appropriate the insights that are accumulated by the tradition. It wants to begin at the beginning but the beginning hides itself behind a screen of history. In the course of the history of Christianity, many believers have (unsuccessfully) tried to shake off the burden of tradition and find a new starting point in an 'unaffected' image of an original Jesus. Direct encounter and indebtedness to tradition remain intertwined. In the preaching and teaching life of a Christian community it is often difficult to distinguish between the insights of the tradition about 'Christ' and the direct impact of the gospel stories about the 'living Jesus'.

The problem takes us back to the duality of *fides qua* and *fides quae*. Living in the tradition means living in that duality. The Christian tradition is not a completed product that can only be accepted or rejected. Every believer is invited to join the traditioning process itself. Living in the tradition is both standing on the shoulders of preceding generations and reliving the dynamic of memory and anticipation that begins at the beginning. Appropriating the Christ-event is both: gratefully entering into an available system of interpretation and at the same time repeating the *qua-quae* duality in each item of interpretation.

Jesus in history

The traditional affirmations of faith about Jesus Christ – born, suffered, died, buried, raised, ascended – do not refer to biographical data that one should accept as 'real history'. They are connecting points for commemoration, invitations to integrate the story that is reflected in those affirmations into one's own life. The confession of faith in Jesus Christ is not a collection of facts but a paradigm for prayer, a model for imitation and identification. Facts were rearranged to that purpose. In other words: the 'historical' Jesus is not available apart from reconstructions performed by commemorating communities. The story that is told about Jesus is shaped by the key elements of that commemorating activity: he is 'the Son of God'; he is 'sent by God to reconcile the world'. The events of Jesus' life are strained by those key elements.

This again implies that faith in Jesus is not in a position to be selective; it cannot, for example, accept Jesus' teaching while rejecting his resurrection. We are confronted with a total package from the very start. The important aspects of Jesus' teaching – about the love of God and neighbour, about losing one's life in order to gain it – are much more than wise lessons by some teacher that can be evaluated for what they are in themselves; rather, they are insights that seek anchorage in human lives as parts of the complete commemoration of Christ.

The appearance of that 'total package' was not a creation out of nothing. It included numerous elements from the time before the Christ-event and from outside its context. The Christ-event took place in a world teeming with religion and philosophy, in which many traditions claimed attention. Much of that imagination was applied to structure the memory of Jesus among the first Christians. In other words: that memory was incorporated into an already-existing history. Only gradually did the Christian tradition receive its independent profile.

Viewed from this angle, the Christ-event is deeply embedded in the Jewish tradition – though obviously the Greek-Hellenistic context also contributed a great deal. The early beginnings of the Christian tradition live, move and have their being primarily in the ecosystem of Judaism; more particularly: in an intense debate between followers of Jesus and those who identify themselves with the Jewish Torah and Prophets. Actually, that debate was never concluded, although it has been dormant for centuries. That it was never totally absent is due to the fact that the literature of the Jewish tradition (the 'Old Testament') was incorporated in the Christian Scriptures at an early stage. In any case, new encounters between Judaism and Christianity in the twentieth century have given the discussion about the relation between the two religions a strong new impulse. Some hold it to be legitimate to consider them as two species of what is basically one 'messianic' tradition. Even without that conclusion, it is obvious that the Christian 'handling' of the self-God-world triad harbours many elements of the Jewish heritage.

Another aspect of the early construction of the Christian tradition that should be considered is the fact that, even though the Scriptures were at some point canonized and thus delineated, a live interaction remains visible between the selected texts and the larger world of scriptures and narratives in which the Scriptures came into being. In the Old Testament, there is interaction of the text with mythical narratives of other cultures and religions and with writings of specific groups within Judaism, for instance apocalyptic sects. In the New Testament, there are all kinds of connections with alternative 'gospels', lost sources, and a large variety of religious writings attributed to early apostles. All this testifies not only to a concentration of Christian tradition (canonization), but also to a fanning out into a wider world of commemoration and reflection. A centripetal force selects writings with a view to identity, and a centrifugal force maintains relations with larger fields of language, religious and cultural worlds and complex patterns of communication in which language develops. Both forces are present in the scriptural writings themselves, and they remain present in the long history of translation and interpretation that constitutes the tradition.

Viewed against the background of this complex network of faith, history and tradition, it is obvious that the texts contained in the Old and New Testaments should be seen as moving within a rich history of memory and anticipation, of imagination and prayer. In other words: the texts themselves are part and parcel of the tradition. They do not constitute an independent body that precedes the tradition or stands above it, and they are certainly not an authoritative source for judgment as to what is and is not acceptable in Christian thought and life. A scriptural authority in that sense does not fit in the view of tradition and commemoration presented in the previous chapters. The dynamic of memory cannot be replaced by an exercise that tests belief and behaviour to texts that are themselves part of an ongoing historical movement. Many biblical texts are temporary solidifications in complex histories of repetition, translation and interpretation – and they should be welcomed and treated according to that quality.

That does not deprive the Scriptures of their unique position. The Scriptures illustrate and document the emergence of the specifically Christian tradition. Their role is to invite participation in a conversation, in which all kinds of stories, reflections, poems and prophecies refer to each other in a dynamic way that never becomes a closed system but keeps a precious and vulnerable process of religious imagination going. The Scriptures are both the birthplace of the Christian tradition and a model for its continuing life.

All these considerations make clear why we do not have access to the 'pure facts' of Jesus' life. But that does not imply that we are prisoners of previous generations in terms of interpretation. We do have access to the *qua-quae* dialectic that has characterized the tradition from the beginning. Commemoration of the Christ-event means making use of that access.

(The discussion about the relation between the 'historical Jesus' and the 'Christ of faith', that occupied theologians for some time after historical reason and religious imagination went their separate ways, could not, for those reasons, be concluded in a satisfactory way. It proved impossible to separate 'pure history' from interpretation, or to construct a difference between a 'real' and an 'imagined' Jesus. In other words, we do not move between the poles of 'pure' history and 'dogmatic' construction, but we are engaged in a permanent conversation between different constructions. The leading question of that conversation is the relation between who Jesus was for the first witnesses and who he is for present day never-ending prayer.)

Leading images: incarnation and resurrection

The traditional affirmations of faith about Jesus Christ contain images that connect his historical presence to God. The Word of God 'became flesh' in him (incarnation). That is a powerful way of saying that the memory of Jesus is an encounter with God and that the contours of God as reconciler, redeemer and creator become tangible in that encounter. The commemoration of Jesus, in other words, is linked to the lifelong

Memory

exercise of prayer as it moves in the triadic relation self-God-world. For the Christian tradition, commemoration and prayer presuppose and include each other.

The difficulty with the concept of incarnation is that it suggests a biological and historical factuality, as if the physical body of Jesus as such were the embodiment of the word of God. The suggestion that incarnation is a quasi-biological event has led to the assumption of several quasi-biological miracles in its periphery, such as 'virgin birth' and 'immaculate conception'. The problem of that biological-historical focus is not so much that it leads to bizarre imagination (although that is the case), but rather that the incarnation is taken out of the context of active commemoration. The human flesh in which the word of God manifests itself should not be identified with the biological organism of the man Jesus, but with the living history that formed around him: the interaction with disciples and other contemporaries, and, following that, the ongoing process of commemoration. The 'flesh' is not Jesus' biological body, but it is the tradition that was created out of the encounter with Jesus. The concept of incarnation is, in this perspective, a quasi-material presentation of the fact that the Christ-event has become part of an ongoing narrative that (in the view of the Christian tradition) is of decisive significance for humankind. That significance is not a consequence of the birth of Jesus as biological event; it is a function of the tradition. To put it differently: the word-becoming-flesh becomes visible in the flesh-becoming-word. Flesh becomes word: that means that this specific human life, this piece of history, becomes history again and again in the lives and the prayers of followers. Never-ending prayer is the space in which the word of God, that appeared in Jesus, lives. That is incarnation.

(A keen dogmatician might object that we are confusing the second and third persons of the Trinity here: 'tradition' should be associated with the outpouring of the Spirit rather than with the epiphany of the Son. That objection is valid if one wants to differentiate between God's actions 'from the point of view of God': 'God revealing himself' versus 'God gathering his flock'. It is less urgent if one reasons from the point of view of the *qua-quae* dialectic: the incarnation assumes 'reality' in the ongoing process of imagination.)

A second leading image in the traditional affirmations about Jesus Christ is his resurrection. The resurrection is the cornerstone of the 'total package' of the Christ-commemoration both in the New Testament and in the history of Christian doctrine, liturgy and art. At the same time, it is extremely problematic for many contemporary believers. The reason for that is that 'resurrection' is not just an image; it is reported as historical fact. For some Christians the acceptance of the pure historicity of that fact is the hallmark of true faith, whereas others are trying to circumnavigate that pure historicity by reading the resurrection-event as a symbolic expression of God's faithfulness to Jesus or as a mythical representation of the ultimate victory of life over death. Both solutions are dead ends. Both remain captive to the either/or realism of modernity and ignore the complexity of a religious imagination that is sparked in and by history.

To address this question, we take our starting point once again in the insight that the commemoration of Jesus deals with a total package that includes the message of his resurrection; the resurrection is not an item that can be regarded as a separate problem. That is especially obvious in the Pauline letters in the New Testament, in which the resurrection is the core and the basis of all that is said about Jesus. We do well to begin our reflection on the resurrection with the rich imagination of those letters: Jesus is elevated into the glory of God, all death and futility have been defeated, life is radically new for those who are 'in Christ'. The Christian tradition reads the gospel stories about Jesus' resurrection through the lenses of that imagination. It is not the miraculous character of the event as such that is brought into focus, but the completely new situation in which the followers of Jesus find themselves on account of that event.

From this point we look back to the gospel stories, and we notice that there, too, the focus is not on a miraculous event but on the 'encounters' of the risen Jesus with his disciples. Those encounters are characterized by doubt and encouragement. The disciples are obviously entering into a new phase of their discipleship and a new kind of relationship with Jesus: Jesus is now 'with God', and the disciples are in a new 'mode of being'. In other words: the tradition that began in a small group of a teacher with his disciples is intensified and brought to life in new, never-ending dimensions.

That is the perspective in which the 'historical fact' of the resurrection ought to be considered. The crucial change in the relation between Jesus and his disciples, that is signalled by the resurrection, is drawn into the story of Jesus' life as the ultimate expression of the 'flesh' that was assumed by the Word of God. It is taken along as 'fact' and at the same time it is the pivotal point at which Jesus' whole life becomes a powerful and life-giving imagination.

(Similar comments can be made about the reported event of the 'ascension into heaven': it is a confirmation of the 'new relationship' inaugurated with the resurrection, and a prelude to the outpouring of the Spirit which highlights the new 'mode of being'. The narratives around the birth of Jesus occupy a comparable position. Like the resurrection, those narratives are positioned between historical fact and religious imagination. Their 'message' is the embeddedness of the Christ-event in an ongoing history, beginning with Israel's prophets and looking forward to peace and justice for all humankind. The actual birth of the infant Jesus is not the core of the narratives, just as the revival of Jesus' dead body is not the core of the resurrection story. At stake is the creation of a tradition that reaches far into the past and far into the future.)

The leading images of incarnation and resurrection signal the transformation of passing history into personally appropriated religious imagination. The factuality of the Christ-event is not thereby denied, ignored or neglected. Jesus is truly 'in history', and so is the construction of the Christian tradition: they have their place in the chain of events from the origin of time to eternity, and in the long pilgrimage of humankind. But the commemoration of Christ claims that a new beginning is made in the Christ-event, directly related to God.

The paradigm of sacrifice

For the early Christian communities, that new beginning was not just an adjustment to new circumstances; it was nothing less than a new perspective on life, on history and on the world. The experience of time itself had changed: prophesies were fulfilled, the 'end of time' was close at hand – in other words: an 'eschatological' freedom had taken over. The domination of law, sin, futility and death was replaced by 'new life in Christ'. In the further development of the Christian tradition, the radical character of this way of remembering the Christ-event subsided, but what remained was the eschatological perspective: the conviction that the Christ-event is a junction of *eschaton* and history. The event stretches the imagination towards the divine completion of world, history and humankind. It reloads never-ending prayer with visions of reconciliation, redemption and creation.

The eucharist, the sharing of bread and wine, is the ritual with which the Christian tradition celebrates this junction-character of the Christ-event. It is impossible to use the terms 'memory' and 'commemoration' in connection with Jesus without referring to the institutionalized memorial of Christ that has been practiced through the ages by nearly all Christian traditions. The eucharist is the focal point of the commemoration of Christ. It evokes the Christ-event and thus announces and inaugurates the time of reconciliation. In a eucharistic celebration, one might say, the original *qua-quae* dialectic of the tradition starts all over again. Each time, the 'junction' is actualized.

That insight is reinforced by the consideration that the eucharist in fact repeats and represents the last meal of Jesus with his disciples, which is reported to have focused on Jesus' promise that the communion with his disciples would continue after his death and his resurrection with a new intensity. That death, moreover, would not be just an accident, but a deliberate sacrifice: Jesus would die on behalf of his friends and thus create the possibility of ongoing sustained communion with him. In other words: the junction between *eschaton* and history that is celebrated in the eucharist is connected to the self-giving of Jesus.

Against this background It is not surprising that the tradition, generally speaking, has been inclined to understand the eucharist as a ritual of sacrifice, more specifically: as a celebration of the sacrifice of Jesus for human salvation. The 'mystery' of the eucharistic sacrifice, as it was (and is) frequently called, is then explained with the argument that Jesus' death was a sacrifice, needed to establish reconciliation between a 'fallen' humankind and an angry God. These images have exercised a considerable influence in the Christian tradition. For many contemporary believers, however, they are no longer convincing. The detailed systematic elaboration of this death-as-sacrifice theme, as if it were a 'contract' between God the Father and God the Son, has mythological features that have little bearing on the problems of guilt and reconciliation in ordinary human lives.

That does not mean that the term 'sacrifice' is out of order in our reflection on the commemoration of Christ. But some clarification is needed. The original religious association with 'sacrifice' is that a killing is necessary to bring about the benevolence of a god. In the Christian narrative, that is not the point. The point is: giving and losing oneself and regaining oneself by grace ('born again') – a self-other dynamic that forms an antidote to the omnipresent reality of guilt. Sacrifice in this sense is entrusting oneself to the 'eschatological' reality of love as the ultimate determining dynamic in the ongoing encounter of self, God and world. It is subordinating one's life to that of others, losing one's life in order to receive it.

The eucharist presents Jesus as a paradigm of giving and receiving, losing and finding, sacrifice and reconciliation. The presence of that paradigm is the 'real presence' of Christ. It is not located in the material elements of bread and wine as such, as if those could bring about a mysterious contact between the believer and Christ. It is true that numerous people understand it that way, and the physical contact with bread and wine often has strong religious connotations. What is questionable about this is that the Christ-paradigm gets to be reduced to a mysterious physical experience, and that many important implications of the memory of the Christ-event are lost. Bread and wine symbolize daily life, and community: the proper context for the celebration of the presence of Christ. But they do not need to be lifted out of daily life in order to function as ritual. It is the other way around: it is the presence of Christ in the ritual of the presented paradigm that 'consecrates' daily life. 'Consecration' in this case means placing that daily life in the perspective of guilt and reconciliation, and 'revealing' God as the reconciler, the redeemer and the creator.

At its deepest level, the eucharist is confession of guilt as response to the paradigm of sacrifice. In the eucharistic commemoration of Christ the rhythm of confession of guilt and reconciliation takes centre stage: as the structure for never-ending prayer, as a pattern for life, as the point of concentration of what the Christian tradition is all about. It celebrates sacrifice as the core image of 'meeting the other' and as the most 'graceful' counter-attack on the omnipresence of guilt.

The coming of the Son of Man

Traditionally, the commemoration of Jesus Christ includes the anticipation of his 'second coming'. According to early confessional statements, he will return once more in full glory, as a triumphant judge. He will manifest himself 'on the clouds'; in other words: he will be unambiguously and inescapably visible for all of humankind. In the course of the centuries, a rich religious imagination has been woven around that article of faith, largely derived from late-Jewish apocalyptic literature. It envisages an end to history; more specifically: an end to a history of injustice, violence and oppression. The coming of 'the Son of Man' will put things right: justice will be done to the oppressed, those who have practised violence will receive eternal punishment. Numerous Christians worldwide cherish some variety of that apocalyptic imagery. The question is: what is its significance in the framework of the commemoration of the Christ-event?

The Christ-event touches a crucial nerve in human life and in the life of humankind: the nerve of guilt and reconciliation. However, the one who is remembered is an outcast, a condemned and executed man, outside the mainstream of history. In the Christian tradition Jesus may have the royal status of the Son of God, but his life's story is not found among the success stories of humankind. That is not only a 'historical fact' (Jesus had to be eliminated as a dangerous revolutionary), but also a central element in the faithful reconstruction of Jesus' life: his humiliating execution is believed to be the pivoting point of history; the 'new beginning' began in the darkness of rejection by the world. That means that the commemoration of Christ still has an open space: the final and decisive appearance of Jesus and of the radical paradigm of reconciliation is still forthcoming; the world still needs to be convinced. That Jesus Christ is the pivotal point of history still needs to 'happen'. In other words: the appearance of Jesus in history is only meaningful in the light of the still-forthcoming event of his vindication: the coming of the Son of Man. Commemorating Jesus, therefore, coincides with the anticipation of his real, definitive coming. It is a celebration that anticipates his all-determining presence.

In the imagination of the Christian tradition, the coming of the Son of Man is related to the whole world. That means that the world – as judged, reconciled, redeemed and created – is present in the commemoration of Christ from the very beginning. Remembering Jesus is not a private affair, as would be the case with groups that cherish the memory of their own 'hero', but it concerns the whole world and all of humankind. That basically implies a universal claim. But it is not a claim that is thrust upon the world from a superior point of view. Rather, it is hidden in the prayer of the commemorating community and in the ritual of confession of guilt and reconciliation. That is the position of the Christian community in the world: not to defend the 'truth' of its faith, but to place itself under the judgment of the Christ-event, together with – and vicariously for – humankind as a whole. That is the way in which it anticipates the coming of the Son of Man.

The 'others' in the world are kept in sight through concentration on the paradigm of sacrifice, of giving oneself, and through focusing on reconciliation beyond all guilty structures. The others are not the people lost in error and darkness that need to be converted, but fellow human beings drawn into the dynamic of never-ending prayer. Deeper penetration into the meaning of the Christ-event creates the space to truly see and embrace others as fellow human beings before God.

8

Anticipation

Human beings are by nature future-directed; existence is impossible without looking ahead. The most simple actions are based on anticipation. Time is tamed by memory but even more so by grasping the not-yet. Planning, expecting, hoping, and also longing for what seems to be impossible – those are basic ingredients of life.

The not-yet structure of human existence has been a constant theme in the previous chapters. Imagination, it was suggested, is kept in motion by the basic intuition of trustworthiness and communication, which means that it is geared towards a situation that is hoped for. The unity of humankind is a vision that transcends all present reality and therefore by definition refers to a future. The self-God-world triad is ultimately anchored in an 'eschatological' view of a reconciling, redeeming and creating God, which means that it is 'hooked' on to something that is not yet fully visible. The memory of Christ is closely linked to the notion of the coming Son of Man. In all these themes the primary focus is not on specific events that are expected to take place in some future, but on the stretching of the imagination, on a self-understanding that relates the self to its largest possible context. The not-yet structure of never-ending prayer is anchored in human existence and it is intensified by the Christian tradition.

The kingdom of God

Because of the not-yet structure of human existence, humankind has always been amenable to images of the future that promise peace, wholeness, salvation, eradication of evil and eternal life. That amenability is not specific for religious traditions, but universally human and of all times. It is linked to a profound sense of the transitory nature of all things and the prospect of complete, fulfilled life. There is a *denouement* ahead. It is sometimes envisioned as a 'paradise': an extension of life but without evil, suffering and death. One meets ancestors and lost loved ones, desires are satisfied, and there is no more illness or need.

But the *denouement* has also been presented as a world to be designed. History abounds with examples of people and groups that have tried to establish a 'kingdom of God' or an ideal state. Since the advent of modernity the idea that a final, meaningful world is within reach has been generally accepted. Ideologies that explain the discrepancy between present suffering and future salvation have highlighted human self-confidence. Religious motives were, and are, not entirely absent in those constructions, though a secular context is presupposed. Even when salvation is described as a historical necessity, it is often presented as a gift of grace, a revelation even, in which the true destiny of humankind is brought to light.

The paradise-version of the *denouement* is still universally popular, but support for the modern design-version seems to be decreasing. The 'grand narratives' of humankind are replaced by the worldwide availability of information and by a global virtual community that introduces the whole world in each context. That is, in a sense, the end of history: substantial changes in the contemporary balance between political, cultural and religious systems are, so it seems, no longer expected.

In this context and against this background, the Christian tradition sustains its prayer for the coming of the kingdom of God. Christians anticipate the enthronement of God as the decisive victory over evil and the final redemption from all suffering. Or, in terms of the previous chapters: the triadic relation of self, God and world steps out of the twilight of uncertainty and ambivalence and finally becomes a face-to-face reality. Although the anticipation of the kingdom has known many diverse expressions, one can safely say that for the tradition as a whole the kingdom of God has always been the great Christian not-yet, and as such one of the strongest sources of faith. Praying, waiting, keeping watch: those words characterize the life of many Christians.

Christians have always believed that the kingdom of God is nearby, close at hand, for the taking, and simultaneously infinitely far away. The kingdom almost forces itself on visible reality; it appears now and then, here and there. Yet it is far away: separate from daily reality, not only because its coming is postponed again and again, but also because it is radically different, it simply does not fit in the way things are organized in the world. It is not clear, therefore, how we should imagine the coming of that kingdom. Is it a divine *coup d'état*, a purge, a creation out of nothing? Is it anarchy or divine dictatorship?

We do well not to focus on the imagination of a perfect society, called 'kingdom of God'. Human imagination cannot produce anything beyond historical and therefore transient forms. Likewise, we do well not to yield to the fundamentalist temptation to speculate (on the basis of religious texts) about the time of the coming of the kingdom. The crucial point is that the kingship of God is the image of a reality in which the divine works of reconciliation, redemption and creation are completely and fully visible, no longer subject to the problems and contradictions of human existence and the history of humankind. As suggested before, the terms reconciliation, redemption and creation do not refer to events that have taken place or will take place; they express the way in which faith qualifies reality. Such qualifying is a choice for a way of thinking and living. Never-ending prayer feeds on the trust that that way is in agreement with things as they are at their deepest and most fundamental level. The question as to whether that ultimate reality will ever become visible and tangible is less urgent than its stubborn anticipation. Anticipating the kingdom means that the not-yet structure of never-ending prayer is mobilized again and again. The advent of the kingdom is 'incarnated' in life itself.

The insight that the kingdom of God is both close at hand and far away expresses two things. In the first place it means that the 'ultimate things' exercise pressure on the 'penultimate things', which is to say that the imagination of an ultimate reality is translated day-to-day in a way of 'meeting the other' and in ordinary daily life. Anticipating the kingdom implies the conviction that the divine work of reconciliation, redemption and creation can be 'incarnated in human flesh'. Waiting for the kingdom is constantly transformed into a hopeful embrace of the world.

Secondly, it means that the relation between God and world is one characterized by judgment. The so-called 'last judgment' occupies a steady place in the Christian imagination. It brings to expression that there is no easy transition between human life and life with God, between guilt and reconciliation. Reconciliation does not cover everything with the cloak of charity. The kingdom of God is a confrontation of the world with what is radically 'other'. In the Christian tradition, it is Christ himself who judges the world and separates those who are eligible for eternal life from those who are not. The pressure of the 'last things', the hopeful embracing of the world – all that is not mere optimism; it implies submission to the permanent and incisive criticism that comes with the memory of Jesus Christ.

Some imagery around the theme of judgment – heaven as eternal bliss, hell as eternal fire – may no longer be convincing. Nonetheless, the contrast between the kingdom of God and the reality of humankind is a serious issue. Human reality is characterized by rationalization of guilt that sustains and hardens a world of conflict. The judgment of the kingdom comes in the form of a permanent question, addressed to selves who involve themselves in the Christian narrative and, through them, to humankind as a whole: Where do you stand? How seriously do you take the paradigm of guilt and reconciliation, and of sacrifice? Judgment is an ultimate question, addressed to all human enterprises, to all designs for a 'better world', and to all efforts to ban evil.

Anticipation of the kingdom can express itself in routine rituals or in the impatient behaviour of those who see themselves as exiles in a hostile world. In between those extremes, never-ending prayer exercises the spirituality of waiting and of openness to everything that is still hidden in the not-yet. It is the spirituality of longing for the definitive meeting of self, God and world.

The unity of humankind

The notion of the unity of humankind – the flourishing of a world in which the need for closure, hostility and defensiveness has been overcome – was introduced and treated in the previous chapters as the implied 'end' of human imagination. It was suggested that it is a basic assumption of imagination that the crossing of frontiers makes sense and that the closing of societies is not final wisdom. That assumption was seen as a form of faith, comparable to the faith in the trustworthiness of being. In other words, imagination as such has a not-yet structure. More strongly, the unity of humankind might be described as a secular *eschaton*, analogous to the kingdom of God. It is, at least, a point where the Christian tradition touches the general narrative of humankind and where its embeddedness is evident.

However, the analogy between 'unity of humankind' and 'kingdom of God' should be treated with some care. On the one hand, the unity of humankind, just like the kingdom of God, is both close at hand and far away. Forms of unity present themselves to the world but they tend to increase tensions instead of encouraging communication. Unity offers itself to humankind, and at the same time it withdraws into a future beyond reach. The unity of humankind is a pressure to which one is invited to respond in small daily actions of frontier-crossing and it is also a judgment on closedness, on the refusal of communication. On the other hand, we should recognize that the notion of the kingdom of God contains aspects that are absent in the notion of the unity of humankind. The Christian tradition holds that faith in the kingdom, or in the unity of humankind, is only imaginable along the lines of guilt and reconciliation. The problem of disunity is therefore deeper than is often imagined. It touches human nature on a more fundamental level. True unity can only be produced through reconciliation, redemption and creation.

At the same time, the unity of humankind highlights problems that are not addressed in the traditional anticipation of the kingdom of God. That is especially true of the violent nature of religious and cultural diversity that has characterized humankind through the ages; of the institutionalization of injustice in present relations among nations and races, of the legacies of hate, handed down through the generations. The consolidation of the 'systems of imagination' in relation to each other – a natural dynamic in the development of humankind – has not only produced diversity but also estrangement, distrust and hostility. In this respect, the notion of the unity of humankind can certainly enrich the 'kingdom of God' tradition.

To be sure, there is a place for 'all nations' in that tradition. At the end of time, the whole world and all of humankind come into view: they flock together, according to ancient prophecies, at the occasion of the enthronement of God, and they will adjust themselves to peace and justice. This 'all nations' aspect of the tradition was revitalized to some extent in the missionary movements of the last centuries, with the aid of the modern view of the world as a coherent field, ready for exploration. Missions were believed to hasten the advent of the kingdom by targeting humankind as a whole. At the same time – that can safely be established in hindsight – the problems of humankind were severely underestimated, both by the missionary movement and by the ambitions of modernity. Cultural, religious, political and economic diversity turned out to be a breeding ground for a highly problematic globalization. That reality needs to be taken seriously in any contemporary reflection on the anticipation of the kingdom of God. The 'unity of humankind', in other words, requests a place in the vocabulary of the Christian tradition.

In this perspective, the anticipation of the kingdom of God obviously implies a serious charge against all structural estrangement, all distrust and hostility that block the unity of humankind. It places the world in the framework of guilt, judgment and reconciliation. One can also say: it presents Jesus Christ in the midst of humankind. That is not necessarily the same thing as global expansion of the Christian community. It is not: defending Christianity as the only true religion, or promoting religion over against secularity. It is: recognizing and presenting the relevance and the promise of the perspective of guilt and reconciliation and the paradigm of sacrifice, in diverse contexts and in communication with diverse cultural and religious traditions – notably where the guilt of humankind is most manifest and tangible. Never-ending prayer includes all of humankind. It cannot resign itself to the prevailing hidden assumption that human beings can only flourish at the expense of each other.

One additional point needs to be considered. The anticipation of the kingdom of God – and, in that perspective, the unity of humankind – implies the acceptance of an unlimited space for the expansion of human imagination. There are many forms of imagination that have been systematically ignored or made invisible by dominant cultures; those, too, will flourish in this space. The Christian tradition does not in advance exclude any of them. It does not have a blueprint for the unity of humankind. What it does have instead is the memory of the Christ-event, the hope for the 'coming of the Son of Man', for judgment, for the revelation of the decisive significance of love, sacrifice, forgiveness and reconciliation. 'On the clouds': that is, visible for all humankind.

(The formulation 'visible for all humankind' betrays a certain exclusivism, as if the Christian tradition has the exclusive right of the possession of 'truth'. Obviously, an exclusivism of sorts is normal for each tradition that takes itself seriously. It is confusing to downplay all truth claims under the pressure of a fashionable pluralism. What is at stake is the upholding of the specific core of the Christian anticipation, not as the exclusively true narrative, but as an incentive to see others as fellow human beings before God, placed in the same dynamic of judgment and reconciliation. For the Christian tradition, that is a 'last' word about humankind, but by no means a conclusion of the discussion.)

The individual not-yet

The not-yet structure of never-ending prayer has very personal aspects. As an existential dynamic, prayer is filled with concern, anxiety, and longing. It moves in the shadow of inescapable death, under the constant pressure of the open questions of self, God and world. It feeds on an imagination that expresses the desire for fulfilment, and on the hope that the praying self, even beyond its own death, will somehow share in that fulfilment.

The awareness of finitude and mortality is a strong impulse for living, for reaching towards a future without ruin and futility. At the same time there is no trivializing of the implacable borderline of death. Death freezes the not-yet, blocks all longing, and labels life retrospectively as contingent, messy and incomplete. The consciousness of mortality, in other words, is double-faced: it encourages and discourages at the same time. The choices that one makes by nature and that determine one's life context are not just nature: they are full of confrontations with mortality. Death is present in the midst of life in countless ways.

The self experiences death not only through its own mortality, but primarily through the death of significant others, of loved neighbours, of victims of illness or violence. Dying begins with the ending of a friendship, the passing of parents or peers, the falling into disuse of trusted ways of life, the betrayal of one's own youthful body that does not keep its promises. In all those cases death not only exemplifies the fact that natural organisms have a natural end, but the fact that the whole business of humankind is full of loose ends, unfulfilled relations, unrepaired damage, undeveloped potential. As the ultimate borderline, death seals and confirms a mortality that works on many different levels in human life. The answer to all that is not immortality but reconciliation.

Never-ending prayer brings the multilayered experience of death together with the commemoration of Christ. That means that the not-yet structure of human existence is placed under the impact of the paradigm of reconciliation and is transformed by it. It is a transformation that redirects the preoccupation with one's own mortality towards a focus on reconciliation. That is a far-reaching and life-encompassing process of conversion, and it requires at least two extensive comments.

In the first place: in the perspective of guilt and reconciliation of Christian faith, selves are not autonomous units but parts of complex networks. They cannot escape one another, there is always interaction, acceptance and rejection, love and hate, reconciliation and guilt. The pressure of the perspective of reconciliation connects human lives to each other and brings them together in an inclusive narrative. The beginning of that narrative lies far before the beginning of each individual life; the completion of it far beyond its end. In other words: the perspective of reconciliation provides selves with a past and a future beyond themselves. The chain of guilt and reconciliation reaches beyond the memory of mortal people. It begins with the unreconciled relations that one leaves behind at the end of one's life, and it ultimately includes all of humankind. The triadic conversation of self, God and world does not come to rest as long as that chain of guilt and reconciliation continues. It remains a never-ending prayer. In any case, one's individual death does not terminate it. One dies 'into humankind'.

In the second place: the core of the Christ-memory is the paradigm of sacrifice, and that paradigm changes the nature of dying. In a sense, of course, dying is a natural process: the human body is an organism for which dying is a necessary aspect of living. The notion of creation adds a dimension to that: selves are called forward from the earth and after some time called back into the earth. In the perspective of creation, life is a destiny, a response to an invitation. The paradigm of self-giving, however, takes one step further. Dying is the completion of a life that has been lived in the perspective of guilt and reconciliation; it is the confirmation of the role that this particular life is playing in the ongoing narrative of reconciliation. The commemoration of Jesus builds a larger narrative around death. That larger narrative is named sacrifice. One dies 'towards the others'.

These two comments show how a preoccupation with death and immortality might be converted into an acceptance of life in which mortality is intertwined with guilt and reconciliation. One does not 'meet God' after death, and 'real life' does not start in the hereafter. A contrast between a contingent, messy and confused life on earth and an eternal perfect life in heaven actually does not belong in the Christian faith, even though it is widespread. The perspective of reconciliation means that the contingency and messiness are to be embraced as the space where God is found. The not-yet structure of existence does not imply that everything is temporary and that 'the real thing' is yet to come. It implies that one lives in hope and confidence; that the not-yet structure is charged with reconciliation. The 'end' is not beyond everything, or in the far future, but it is hidden in the world as the dynamic of guilt and reconciliation, and it is 'lived' in never-ending prayer.

Life-death-life

It is a universal human experience that life is 'towards death'. How does that relate to the stake of never-ending prayer that life is 'towards love'? We have considered that human lives are interconnected in numerous ways, and that this interconnection ultimately includes all of humankind. Life flows into lives of others in the ongoing mobility of human community. To put it more strongly: human beings belong to a network of grace, because they are brought forth as well as brought home by others. The meaning of life depends on what others do with it. Christian faith holds that that network ultimately rests in the grace of God. In that perspective, the pursuit of individuality, the securing of one's own body and soul, the clinging of the self to itself – though it is part of human nature – leads astray, to the extent that it can ignore or even deny the narrative of guilt and reconciliation. The alternative is: designing one's life in such a way that its dominating theme becomes handing over, giving away. Then dying is the fulfilment of life instead of its denial or annihilation. Learning to live from grace is learning to die. The art of dying is: to sound the theme of losing oneself in the midst of life. The art of dying is not the daily exercise of convincing oneself of finitude, but the daily exercise of losing oneself.

Of course that does not mean that each life that takes the perspective of guilt and reconciliation seriously should end in concrete self-sacrifice. And certainly not that the numerous victims of hatred, violence and injustice should be idealized as great examples of reconciliation. Death appears in many forms, and most of those give no occasion for religious romanticism; to the contrary, they illustrate that the world is 'lost in guilt'. Nevertheless: it is wrong to say that dying as such is the great loss, the final elimination from the game of life. Dying is the final step of a life that loses itself and as such becomes part of the larger coherence of guilt and reconciliation. In that sense, dying is the confirmation of a life that entrusts itself to the vitality of sacrifice, to the receiving and giving love that reveals itself as the decisive energy in reality. Dying is like life itself: falling into the earth to flourish, and bearing fruit in the reality of God – no longer dependent on the tools with which humans again and again seek to secure their body and soul.

In the Christian tradition, the notion of 'dying with Christ' or 'dying in Christ' has always played an important role. It can be interpreted to mean as much as: identifying with the paradigm of sacrifice, recognizing the way of Jesus in one's own life story. Even the somewhat bizarre stories about saints who experience the scars of Jesus in their own bodies (the *stigmata*) might be understood in that way. They underline that also the relation with one's own mortal and dying body can be part of a life that 'gives itself'. Selves can reconcile themselves to their own ailments in a more fundamental way than just the acceptance of inevitable decline. That is also true for one's life history with its many moments of guilt and reconciliation. It is taken up into never-ending prayer and the anticipation that it cherishes. The anticipation is not: waiting for a particular *denouement* in which everything will be changed all of a sudden, but it is: becoming part of the ongoing narrative of reconciliation, redemption and creation. That narrative does not end with death but includes dying. The art of dying is: identifying oneself with it.

Meanwhile it is obvious that reflections such as these do not fully satisfy religious imagination: it needs more certainty about life after death. Images of an everlasting afterlife are probably as old and as widespread as humankind itself. Imagination tries to uphold the not-yet structure of existence against the threat of death and to overrule the inescapability of the end. It is natural for imagination to do so, because it is based on the intuition of the unity of reality of which the knowing and observing self is a part, and that unity is larger than any 'incidental' piece of life. For imagination, death is a starting point for ongoing activity: the scenery changes but the play goes on. The universally human longing for redemption from suffering and brokenness and the unbearable certainty of death only stimulate that imagination.

Nevertheless, practically all images of an afterlife are characterized by a certain awkwardness: nothing sensible can be said about what awaits human beings after death. There is no knowledge or experience about postmortal consciousness. Near-death experiences or physical speculations about other dimensions do not change that. Besides, there is no image about life after death that does not run into contradictions: all human experiences with bliss and fulfilment are necessarily linked with finitude. Resurrected bodies or immortal souls are very difficult to imagine.

What light can be shed on the imagination of an afterlife by the commemoration of Christ and the anticipation of the kingdom of God? The first thing that should be said about this is that Christian faith is not the assurance of a life after death, nor the guarantee of a simple passage to new life. Death is real death. At the same time, prayer is the space in which the open questions of self, God and world lose their ambivalence, and in which the precariousness of existence and the unbearability of death are overruled by the prospect of an eternal realm of love. In that perspective, dying is not falling prey to annihilation, but a specific form of interaction with reality: an interaction of surrender and love, that can, retrospectively, renew life.

In this perspective, images of an afterlife, of a 'heaven', a 'life with God', a reunion with lost loved ones, can become sidetracks or even false guides. A preoccupation with afterlife can result in the neglect of the larger framework in which faith places living and dying, because everything is reduced to the personal-existential problem of dying and living. Having said that, however, we should add that a rejection of all images of a life hereafter would impoverish the life of faith. Such images can be expressions of never-ending prayer: a cautious effort to catch in word and image that the relation with God continues beyond death. Prayer places life in God's hands, not just at the moment of dying but throughout. Perhaps one can say that the word 'afterlife' is unfit or even misleading. It wrongly suggests a form of life that replaces present life and comes 'after', whereas the Christian tradition would be inclined to speak of a life that encompasses the present finite life from beginning to end and takes it to a higher level. The connection between finite life and that higher level is precisely never-ending prayer.

It should be added that this 'higher-level life' still consists of the triadic relation of self, God and world. The ultimate end of life is not a relation between self and God in which the world is left aside or cast off. That would be a religious form of resistance against being-in-the-world, and as such also against dying. Without 'world' (and without dying) a relation between self and God has no substance; self and God could not even be defined in relation to each other. All efforts to imagine a 'soul' without body or world – a soul that would be united with God after death – are diversions from the fundamental given that there is one reality, inexhaustible yet saturated with divine love. In other words: never-ending prayer is heaven on earth.

9

Mission

Mission is the life of the tradition as it touches the dynamic of humankind. It is the reverse side of embeddedness, signifying the active relation of the Christian narrative with world and context. Together with memory and anticipation, it belongs to the inner movement of never-ending prayer, while at the same time expressing its outwardness. Mission is not the application of tradition, nor the export of a ready-made product to foreign territory; it is the tradition's original momentum towards the ends of the earth.

To (re)define mission in this way is a precarious undertaking. The term 'mission' needs to be recaptured and delivered from a still-widespread association with the organized expansion of Christianity, generally called the modern western 'missionary movement'. Diverse and multicoloured as it was, this movement was characterized by a one-way traffic from (western) Christian to (non-western) non-Christian contexts, by a spirituality of conquest, and by an underestimation of the stubbornness of religious and cultural plurality. Although traces of the movement can still be discerned in various organized 'missionary' initiatives, its general thrust came to an end with the passing of colonialism, a profound change in global relations, and the self-assertion of the 'non-western world'. As a consequence, the term 'mission' lost its traditional habitat and came to designate a large variety of Christian practices, from social action to hospitality of communities. In spite of all this, it is undeniable that the term has had strong credentials in the Christian tradition from its very beginning. For that reason it is worthwhile to recapture it as a basic theological notion that does not merely refer to Christian practices but, more fundamentally, to the inescapable presence of 'the world' in Christian imagination as such.

(In twentieth-century missionary thinking, the formula *Missio Dei* has been proposed as reference to the conviction that all missionary activity derives from God's all-encompassing world-directedness; 'mission' is then seen as a movement 'within the Trinity'. The formula not only suffers from a lack of theological clarity; it has also become an excuse to label a large variety of movements, both Christian and secular, as 'mission'.)

Missionary dynamic

The Christian tradition is embedded in the history of humankind. At the same time it addresses that history from a specific point of view: a point of view that is rooted in the historical Christ-event. As that event is commemorated as a junction of history and eschatology, the point of view locates itself in a sense outside or 'above' history. The Christian narrative, in other words, flows into the human narrative while at the same time rewriting it 'from the outside'. The two narratives are entangled but only in the unity of humankind will they finally coincide. In the meantime, the rewriting continues through the movements of memory and anticipation, both in selves and in communities. Those movements have an impact, not only on the selves and communities concerned but also on their contexts. Behind the reality of embeddedness lies the reality of active information, confrontation and transformation. That is missionary dynamic.

It is, of course, an oversimplification to place the 'Christian' and the 'human' narrative over against each other as two distinct entities. In fact, the human narrative consists of an immense variety of cultural and religious traditions and socio-political contexts, and each instance of impact by the Christian narrative has different connotations and results. Nor, obviously, is the Christian tradition itself a uniform matter. It may already be unwarranted to speak of the Christian tradition in the singular, much less does it seem justified to refer to 'missionary dynamic' as one reality. To the contrary, it is precisely that dynamic that transforms the Christian narrative again and again into a confusing plurality. The singularity of the Christ-event may draw the world into a certain uniformity as 'world'; the world itself virtually forces the Christ-event into a plurality of expressions and interpretations. That tension characterizes the Christian tradition in a fundamental way. To speak of mission, therefore, summons the basic problem of dispersing and gathering.

The 'reverse side of embeddedness' presents itself in numerous ways and on different levels. It can be recognized in individual conversions, in the emergence of new faith communities, in the institutionalization of churches, in political decisions, in efforts to sustain a particular lifestyle or culture, in the invention of rituals, in artistic expression, even in ephemeral responses. All those varieties of visibility become marking points that identify the tradition and simultaneously function as starting points for ongoing missionary dynamic. Those marking and starting points should not prematurely be called signs of victory in a conquest that produces fragments of a 'kingdom of God'. The missionary dynamic is not a triumphal progress but rather a running commentary, a constant stimulus for the reorientation of life. It is by definition unfinished business; it keeps exploring deeper layers in the self, more aspects of individual and communal life, more world and more future. The memory and anticipation associated with the Christ-event 'invade' human life step by step; they do produce visible forms, systems and institutions, but these are by definition provisional. The dynamic is never-ending.

Of course, mission is not a random movement that moves by itself as if it were an impersonal energy. First of all, there is a logic to it, that is determined by two poles: the Christ-event and the eschatological perspective. The logic may at times be hidden or obscured behind motives of propaganda and self-preservation, but it will manifest itself again and again if there is a sustained feedback with the dynamic of memory and anticipation. Secondly, it moves through persons (and communities) who consciously engage themselves with the tradition and thus, implicitly or explicitly, show the extent to which they have been changed by it.

Traditional expressions for that personal missionary engagement are 'proclaiming Christ' or 'spreading the message'. Although those expressions are widely used and generally accepted, the problem is that they do not sufficiently reflect the eschatological logic. That logic places the world in the framework of guilt, judgment and reconciliation. That means that the missionary dynamic aims at recognizing and presenting the relevance and the promise of the perspective of guilt and reconciliation and the paradigm of sacrifice. Rather than defending Christianity as the only true religion or striving for the global expansion of the Christian community, its business is the introduction of the active commemoration of the Christ-event in diverse contexts – notably where the guilt of humankind is most manifest and tangible. Those contexts can be personal lives, social structures, situations or histories. Presenting Christ in the midst of humankind, in other words, is not presenting an answer or a solution; rather, it is engaging in a learning process in which Christ is (re)discovered again and again. The encounter with the

Christ-event is continuously repeated; the encounter with 'the world' elicits the original *qua-quae* dialectic that has fed the tradition from the beginning. That is missionary dynamic.

Concentrating the tradition as a whole in a confessional formula or in a 'message' as the point of departure for 'missionary activity', by contrast, runs the risk of passing over and neglecting that basic missionary dynamic. Missionary dynamic in fact precedes any definition of the message.

Dispersing

In its missionary shape, the Christian tradition disperses itself; it necessarily moves in the direction of plurality. It is important to recognize that plurality and diversity are not unfortunate side-effects in a one-directional history of Christianity, but original characteristics. Plurality is the necessary outcome of the dynamics of tradition itself. The triad of memory, anticipation and mission as it materializes in the world implies dispersal. Dispersing is the explosion of imagination out of the junction of history and eschatology that is located in the Christ-event. It takes the world seriously from the eschatological point of view (the 'ends of the earth'). It is full of promise.

This basic fact is reflected in the diversity of contemporary global Christianity. All efforts to present Christianity as a unity, however necessary they are, cannot obscure or overrule the evidence that Christian diversity is original and never-ending. It would be short-sighted to attribute it to modern globalization only: to the contrary, the diversity reveals, in hindsight, that it has been characteristic of the history of Christianity from the beginning. The history of western Christianity is in fact a constant battle between persisting diversification and self-appointed centres of unity – a battle in which 'unity' frequently appears to have been on the losing side.

In spite of this evidence, a widely shared presupposition in the approach to the problem of plurality and unity is that Christian plurality is a secondary by-product of an originally given line of unity. According to that (mistaken) presupposition, Christianity came from the Near East to Europe; though constantly plagued by heresies and schisms (particularly the Reformation) it remained a more-or-less recognizable whole; it then expanded to the 'new world', and after that to the rest of the world, mainly through missionary endeavour. In that frame of thought western Christianity is implicitly identified as the mother of global Christianity and as its inescapable preliminary stage. However, widespread as it may be, this view needs to be reconsidered.

The assumption that global Christianity is an 'appendix' to western Christianity met with increasing criticism in the wake of the worldwide ecumenical movement in the course of the twentieth century. Two things were instrumental for that criticism: the fact that statistics made clear that Christianity in the southern hemisphere rapidly outgrew northern Christianity on its own strength; and the discovery of the importance of local histories and local agents for the emergence and growth of 'new' Christian expressions. The term 'World Christianity' came into use as a corrective of the pervasive conviction that Christianity, even in its global expansion, somehow remained 'western-based'. The Christian tradition, in other words, was deterritorialized.

What is fundamentally at stake in that deterritorialization is a paradigm shift, the consequences of which are only gradually dawning on mainline western Christians. That shift implies much more than just taking 'new' Christian expressions of faith seriously. It implies reconsidering traditional views of western-centreed Christian history. More strongly: it produces an important *nuance* in the concept of tradition itself. Three points call for attention here.

First of all, the traditional linear view, according to which the Christian tradition first developed in the western world and afterwards in other continents, is not only historically wrong, it also mistakenly supposes that plurality of forms and beliefs only gradually emerged in relation to an original 'centre'. In fact, the history of Christianity was polycentric from the very beginning. Dispersal, rather than unity, was the reality of the tradition as soon as it presented itself. Contemporary global Christianity shows that it is short-sighted to set up one specific history as the unquestioned frame of reference for a view of 'the' Christian tradition. That tradition does not consist of one main road and many sideroads; instead, there are multiple histories.

Secondly, the dispersal of World Christianity leads to new attention for local histories instead of age-long lines of continuing historical influence. It shifts the focus from what is received from preceding generations and foreign contexts to what is created by contemporaries – analogous to the way in which the 'history of missions' shifts the focus from foreign missionaries to local converts. What counts is the fresh confrontation with local culture and religion, rather than faithful identification with the inheritance. Inevitably, this approach in turn influences the way in which western Christianity comes into view: here too, local encounters between the tradition and existing forms of culture and religion appear to be a more promising focus of attention than the measure of conformity with the past. The history of western Christianity is itself a complicated process of specific accommodations and variations, in which the tradition is not 'given' beforehand as an unchanging identity. Viewed in that perspective, even the 'old' Christianity of the West is full of opportunities for new developments.

Thirdly, the concept of tradition itself calls for reconsideration, at least to some extent. The usual model of a narrative or a structure that is passed on through time no longer holds a monopoly position. There is a second model: that of a map showing a network of connections that do not necessarily refer back to a common specific origin. Vertical, chronological lines are combined with, if not replaced by, horizontal relations between simultaneous phenomena. To explain the difference between the two models, some use the metaphor of the *rhizome* (a biological structure of underground roots) as a substitute for the metaphor of the tree. The image of the rhizome implies that tradition acquires features of a nomadic system of expansion, in addition to its usual interpretation as a particular structuring of time that is handed down through the generations. Applied to the theme of dispersing, the rhizome model would imply that plurality is not (only) the result of the diversification of an original unity, but (also) of the engagement with contemporary forms of life (contextualization). That engagement is a repetition of the original dynamic of dispersing, rather than the product of an ongoing linear history.

Gathering

To characterize the missionary dynamic of the Christian tradition, the notion of dispersing is necessary but not sufficient. Without 'gathering' as its reverse side, it is not complete. As dispersing is the explosion of imagination out of the Christ-event, gathering refers back to its source and is intent on continuing identity. Gathering does not precede dispersing, nor is dispersing a prelude to gathering; the two dynamics are simultaneous. Memory and anticipation of the Christ-event produce dispersal as they are activated in the world; but simultaneously they draw people together as they keep referring back to the original event. That 'drawing force' expresses itself in never-ending prayer and in rituals such as the eucharist. Without the dynamic of gathering, the Christian tradition would have no recognizable form or content.

Obviously, the prime example of gathering is the formation of communities of followers of Jesus Christ. But we might just as well think of the process of individual conversion. A self is 'gathered' into the Christian faith, meaning that more and more aspects of its life are reinterpreted and 're-lived' as part of the ongoing activity of memory and anticipation. The self-God-world triad, which constitutes the 'stuff' of the self's life, is gradually permeated by the implications of the Christian tradition. This happens gradually, because an individual life is by definition linked to others, to its context and to the world in numerous ways, and not all those links are simultaneously transformed when that life begins to be touched by faith. There is always more 'life', more 'world' to be illuminated by the Christian narrative, even within one particular self. In this perspective, individual conversion is identical with never-ending prayer. It is the incorporation of a human life into an encompassing faith-narrative, and that is by definition unfinished business. In that unfinished business, gathering and dispersing go hand in hand.

Analogously, the formation of a community of believers is the gathering of selves and their contexts under the aegis of the Christian tradition. This, too, is by definition never complete but always in motion: the gathering reaches out to a fuller inclusion of the lives already touched and to the 'world' at large. The gathering dynamic introduces a concentration in the boundlessness of dispersal – a concentration that implies ordering of communal life, leadership and concern for continuity. Principally, that concentration does not limit, replace or end the dispersing; to the contrary, it is supposed to refer constantly to the original encounter with the Christ-event from which the dispersing springs, and to stimulate the ongoing movement of the tradition.

This way of phrasing, however, already indicates that the preservation of a careful balance between dispersing and gathering, although crucial for the ongoing movement of the tradition in the context of the narratives of humankind, is a heavy challenge. History shows that the tension between the drive of ongoing contextualization and pluralization on the one hand and the desire to establish centres of unity, oversight and control on the other has often been explosive. Obviously, the original duality of dispersing and gathering becomes more difficult to maintain as the levels of institutionalization become more complex.

The history of the ecumenical movement in the twentieth century reflects that difficulty in a special way. This movement originated in a strong desire to present a common witness and a visibly unified Christian presence in a disintegrating world, as a sign of hope for humankind. It was a modern movement, in the sense that it responded to the problems of increasing globalization and to the suggested advance of a 'unity of humankind'. Under its umbrella, a large variety of models of unity was considered. 'Gathering' was understood as the uniting of the people of God around the world into a 'single body'.

But how could 'unity' as a concrete project be brought to the attention of an institutionally divided Christianity, in which the challenge of dispersing and gathering was already being met in so many different ways? Obviously, a common reference to Jesus was not sufficient to achieve this. Would it be possible to designate an original form of Christianity in the first centuries as normative? Should 'tradition' be understood as a metahistorical reality that encompasses all separate Christian traditions and ultimately binds them together? Is work on doctrinal consensus about specific aspects of the Christian faith a trustworthy road to choose? Or is 'unity' to be understood as given with common spiritual experience, joint diaconal service, and combined battle against global manifestations of injustice? What is a realistic degree of visibility for unity?

A persistent element in this whole area of discussion has been the focus on the mutual recognition of ministry among the different churches, more specifically: on the possible acceptance of the historic episcopate as the basic structure of unity. It is an attractive approach if one gives priority to the institutionalization of the tradition. However, against the background of the sketched duality of dispersing and gathering it has serious shortcomings – shortcomings that in turn exemplify the limitations of the unity project as a whole.

The approach presupposes a 'strong' concept of ministry. That means that the ministry is seen as responsible not only for keeping the community together (chiefly by celebrating the eucharist), but also for guarding the content of the tradition and its orderly transmission. In other words, the continuity of the ministry is practically put on a par with the continuity of the tradition as such. A consequence of this is that the concern for the continuity of the given church body is placed before any 'missionary' concern, which is then automatically regarded as secondary. With that, the approach betrays its dependence on a linear view of tradition, in which historical continuity takes precedence over contextual development.

What is in danger of getting lost in the unity project as a whole is the balance of the missionary dynamic, given with the Christ event. Gathering is a crucial part of that dynamic, but, separated from dispersing, it becomes concerned with survival of existing structures, as if these as such embody the event. More important: to safeguard gathering as the main business of the tradition is eschatologically premature. The gathering of the people of God is not an end in itself but a provisional alignment for the expectation of a final gathering that concerns humankind as a whole. The unity of the church refers to the unity of humankind. When that reference is lost, when the unity of humankind becomes secondary to the unity of the church, the right order of eschatology and ecclesiology gets lost, and the coherence of the Christ-event itself is in jeopardy.

This is not to downplay the significance of unity, or of ministry for that matter. Concern for unity is essential for gathering, and so is the concern for an adequate and consistent ministerial structure. But the point of ministry is not self-preservation; it is the creation of spaces for the ongoing celebration of the junction between history and eschatology that presents itself in the Christ-event, and the ongoing activation of the memory and anticipation connected to it. In that perspective, 'unity' among the different Christian traditions is not served by any superstructure or doctrinal compromise. It is served by common efforts to refer to that origin and to challenge all who profess allegiance to the Christian tradition to give account of the way in which that beginning is honoured. Apostolicity – the faithfulness of the tradition to its origin – rests in that common account, rather than in structural guarantees.

In the ecumenical movement, the (common) celebration of the eucharist is often regarded as a last achievement, as the final attainment of unity. A consequence of this view is that such a celebration should be postponed until all negotiations about doctrine and ministry are rounded off successfully. But the eucharist is not the consummation of unity, it is its instrument. It brings people together into what is the most fundamental movement of the Christian community. It is not the seal of an accomplished project but the repeated beginning of what the community is all about. It revives the dialectic of *fides qua* and *fides quae*. It creates space for memory, anticipation, and never-ending prayer.

Church

In all its diversity, continuity and discontinuity, the church remains the most consistently visible reference to the Christian tradition. The church witnesses to the existence and ongoing movement of the tradition in an institutional way. The institution may not produce or control the tradition, it serves it by maintaining a certain discipline of community, the celebration of rituals, and the storage of experiences and insights of previous generations of believers. It reflects the missionary dynamic of the tradition and in turn seeks to stimulate it.

This cautious definition implies a critical comment on the tendency in large parts of Christianity to place the church at the centre of the history of salvation. When that happens, the church is seen as the rightful embodiment of the Christ-event, and as the source and supervisor of the worldwide dynamics of dispersing and gathering. One of the problems of this church-centred approach is that faithfulness to the Christian tradition is easily confused with faithfulness to a specific contextual community-structure and its linear continuity. More serious, however, is the implication that the appearance of the church is more-or-less identified with the appearance of Christ, and that the dynamics of memory, anticipation and mission are understood as properties of the church rather than as conditions that make its emergence possible.

These problems can be avoided when the Christian narrative is understood as an eschatological dynamic that is directed to the world and to humankind as a whole, and the church is understood as reference to that dynamic. The church can only be appreciated for what it is when it is related to the universal framework of the divine action of reconciliation, redemption and creation. Again: eschatology precedes ecclesiology.

Only with this critical comment in mind is it possible to appreciate the eucharist as the visible form *par excellence* of memory and anticipation. The ritual of the eucharist is not primarily a confirmation of the authority of the church to 'represent' the Christ-event. It is the symbolic concentration of what is essential in the encounter with Christ; it is the reconstruction of the crucial moments of his life, death and resurrection. That reconstruction makes room for confession of guilt and never-ending prayer. Confession of guilt means: becoming aware of the framework of guilt in which human life exists and accepting and reproducing the context of reconciliation and sacrifice in which human life is 'reborn'. Celebration of the eucharist means liberating oneself from the routine of everyday life and entering the triadic movement of self, God and world in the perspective of the remembered Christ.

Everything the church is and does in terms of community, ministerial structure, liturgical celebration, pastoral care and diaconal service can and should be understood as proceeding from the eucharist. Liturgy is built around the eucharist; it employs a wide range of human self-expression (from immense joy to bitter complaint) for the emotional and spiritual aspects of the encounter with Christ. Pastoral care is the concern for selves in their personal never-ending prayer, for the measure in which they 'gather' the various aspects of their lives into the dynamic of memory and anticipation. It helps selves to move to a level of life where self-reflection, guilt and reconciliation are constitutive factors. Pastoral care takes place in personal contacts, but also in communal functions such as ritual and proclamation. Likewise, diaconal practice emerges – almost as a matter of course – out of the eucharistic sharing of bread and wine. This practice of sharing is continued in the exchange of concrete signs of compassion, and in the recognition of material need in the immediate context. Both pastoral care and diaconal service cultivate and practice an 'eschatological' vision of human life; implicitly and explicitly they 'proclaim' the significance of that vision for selves and communities. They drink from the same (eucharistic) well.

That does not mean that they remain purely ecclesial activities. By their very dynamic they constantly cross the line between church and 'world'. Liturgy engages the culture of the context. Pastoral care for selves explores unexplored territory in the self: pieces of 'world' in the self not yet touched by faith. Diaconal service meets 'the world' as a whole in the need of individuals. In other words: the eucharist connects the church with the context and as such with the wealth of human narratives that surround the specific Christian tradition. As suggested before, this connection is basically missionary in nature. Its aim is not to merge with secular welfare practices or to replace them, but to 'remind' humankind of the perspective of guilt, reconciliation and sacrifice.

In modern secularized societies, organized state welfare has, to a large extent, taken over the institutionalized church practices of pastoral care and diaconal service. Likewise, 'secular' psychological and social theories have influenced theological thinking about selves and communities. It is obvious that these developments have helped and stimulated churches in their outreach to society, but also that they raise identity-problems and questions with regard to the specific nature of the presence of the church in the world. Those questions can only be dealt with in a productive way if they are brought in relation with the missionary dynamic from which the church emerges and by which it exists. A 'missionary church' is not a community that tries to recruit new members by making itself attractive to its context, but a community in which the original missionary dynamic shines through all its practices. 'Mission' is not a separate activity next to pastoral care and diaconal service; it is the *raison d'être* of the church as such.

To summarize: the distinction between church and world has a twofold character. On the one hand the church is a distinct community, marked by the decision of those who consciously join the pilgrimage of the Christian narrative through humankind. On the other hand it is eschatologically fluid: never definitively closed, permanently referring to the unity of humankind.

World

World is the summary of everything that matters. It is not an object of observation or knowledge that can be externalized to the self; rather, it is permanently presupposed in the self-God-world triad. In relation to the self, the world is history, evolution and cosmos. In relation to God, the world is the space of reconciliation, redemption and creation. The Christian tradition reconstructs the self-God-world triad as a perspective of faith, hope and love.

In traditional Christian language, by contrast, the world is generalized and objectified as external to God's action: it is the object of creation, reconciliation and redemption, and as such also the address of a missionary enterprise that announces God's kingdom. In this language, 'world' remains unspecified; it comes to mean everything that is not God, and – in missionary thinking – everything that is at the receiving end of the line of salvation that is drawn through history. It has a negative identity. More strongly: 'world' often becomes a mere rhetorical device that leaves actual self-God-world experiences unaccounted for. There are traces here of a premodern dualism but also of a typically modern view of the world-as-a-project, of the world as a field to be possessed and explored. All that was (and still is) useful to support the spirituality of conquest that was characteristic of the modern missionary movement. For that reason alone, some rethinking is in order.

When 'world is the summary of everything that matters', in other words: when the world is not objectified but experienced and understood as the never-ending series of contexts in which we live, move and have our being, then it becomes virtually impossible to conceive of the world as a whole. One would need a God's-eye view, or, in terms of human imagination, eyes of faith and an eschatological perspective. That perspective, so the Christian tradition holds, is reconciliation. Christian faith means integration in the world in a specific way, rather than placing Christians in a distinct position over against it. In the eschatological perspective of reconciliation, the world (and life in all its dimensions) becomes the theatre of creation and redemption, rather than the 'other' reality. Reconciliation is an image, a vision in which humankind reaches its destiny. It is a vision by means of which the Christian tradition permanently challenges and renews itself.

Against this background it must be emphasized that the missionary dynamic of the Christian narrative is not a foreign element that 'comes into the world' in the same way as the Christ-event itself, but that it is born out of the appropriation of that event. That appropriation – memory, anticipation and mission – occurs within a pluriform field of imagination that is already there. In this way, the Christian tradition takes its place among the many (religious and non-religious) images that constitute the pilgrimage of humankind. More specifically: the religious imagery of the divine action of reconciliation, redemption and creation activates and stimulates the process of imagination as such. It does so by offering a specific way to visualize what imagination is all about. Seen in this way, mission is an appeal to the promise inherent to humankind.

In its eschatological ambition, the Christian tradition positions itself among the many systems of religious imagination, not primarily as a contestant for religious truth, but as a constant interference that focuses on intensifying and radicalizing the self-God-world triad. It invites humankind to join it in a learning process in which the relevance and the impact of the Christ-event is rediscovered in ever-changing contexts, so that the world may become truly 'world': reconciled, redeemed, created. That is not a claim that is thrust upon the world from a superior point of view; rather, it is a wager, an investment in hope.

When mission is understood as the engagement in and the invitation to a learning process, it implies more than the sharing of knowledge or the introduction of new images as such. Rather, it is a careful reading of contexts in which the business of being human might be enlightened by wider perspectives, notably the perspective of guilt and reconciliation; and it is an investigation into the ways in which the memory of Christ might come to life in those contexts. In this sense, mission is the 'sharing of world' in eschatological perspective.

That is not the same thing as a contest for religious truth. To be sure, in its journey through the various contexts of humankind the Christian tradition constantly encounters other traditions. It finds itself in numerous different cultural configurations and religious spheres of influence – both on the level of everyday popular religion and on the level of more developed religious systems, in which age-long traditions have left their marks. Obviously, the globalized world provides many occasions for dialogue between Christianity and 'other religions'. Such dialogue is undoubtedly very useful in the larger context of the arena of human imagination: it increases knowledge and stimulates critical reflection on one's own tradition. But it is not mission. Mission is: raising the 'Christ-question' in the 'worlds' of human beings. Of course, that will involve serious attention for the cultural and religious shaping of those 'worlds' – but not with the intention to prove those wrong or to replace them with elements brought in from other contexts.

The aim of mission is not the victory of the Christian tradition as 'system of truth'; it is not even the vindication of religious imagination as a tool of salvation. It is the flourishing of the triad self-God-world; and that is the fulfilment of the intuition that is inherent to the activity of human imagination as such. In eschatological perspective, religion is an auxiliary structure and not a goal in itself. Mission reaches beyond it, even as it expresses itself in the words and images of the Christian tradition. Never-ending prayer is prayer in which the world comes to itself.

A Personal Epilogue

This book reflects half a century of theological existence – an existence that bears the marks of radical changes in the world scene. It was a time of profound shifts in global relations and also a time in which the age-long affinity between the Christian tradition and western culture seemed to come to an end. My theological journey began in the relatively safe context of the alliance between Christianity and modernity that allowed for a more-or-less open dialogue with science and philosophy. That safety no longer exists. In a world of ongoing secularization, postmodern thinking and recurring interreligious and intercultural clashes, the modern narrative of the world-encompassing self-confidence of western Christianity is no longer credible. That narrative had provided me with a home to grow up in but that home has become uninhabitable. This book reflects both: the security of the early years and the later experience of exile. It testifies to the richness and relevance of the Christian tradition as well as to the need to rethink much of its heritage.

Two questions have remained dominant during my journey. The first concerns the nature of faith. What does it mean that people hold on to 'truths' about God, world and themselves? Do these truths come from a supernatural source or are they the outcome of human struggles with life and death? What is the relation between relative and absolute, between reason and revelation, history and eschatology? Are the liberal and the confessional-orthodox approaches to these issues irreconcilable? The second question is about the world: what are humankind and nature in the eyes of faith, and what is the position and function of the community of believers in the vast space of cultures and religions? Both the faith-question and the world-question are related to the theme of secularization, which was hotly debated in my student days. Many of us were convinced that we should interpret the (as we thought irreversible) process of secularization as a legitimate liberation from religious and ecclesial structures, as those structures obscured the true 'worldly' meaning of the Christian Gospel. And it was the world, rather than the church – humanity, rather than religion – that was the theatre of the *Missio Dei*.

Important guides in my early years were Hans Hoekendijk, Dietrich Bonhoeffer and Rudolf Bultmann, and – in the background – Søren Kierkegaard and Martin Heidegger. They helped me, each in his own way, to search beyond the given structures of religion, church and culture for an ultimate point of reference, and thus to radicalize the faith-question. Hoekendijk in particular, with his stubborn insistence that in the theological order of things 'world' precedes 'church' and eschatology precedes ecclesiology, provided a framework for the further elaboration of both the faith-question and the world-question. He was joined by Arend van Leeuwen, Ernst Bloch and Jürgen Moltmann with their interpretation of history as a dynamic of hope and revolution. Faith in God implies the dethronement of many lesser gods, including gods that are dear to many Christians.

Next came my encounter with American 'neo-orthodoxy' during my studies at Yale University Divinity School. Richard Niebuhr symbolized the effort to create a synthesis between theological liberalism and confessionalism, or, more precisely: the effort to find a middle course between Friedrich Schleiermacher, who constructed theology on the basis of human religiosity, and Karl Barth, who gave unconditional priority to the sovereign word of God. American neo-orthodoxy – other than European dialectical theology – held that the reality of God could be understood within religious and (social) ethical experience, but it wanted to correct an all-too-simple liberalism by emphasizing a critical distance between God and world. Faith in God is an existential adventure, requiring much religious and moral effort; if faith is taken seriously it is 'radical' in the sense that it wages a constant battle with 'smaller' forms of religion and restricted 'closed' visions of life that are unable to appropriate the ever-transcending universality of God. What attracted and stimulated me was the relocation of 'revelation' in the context of actual human dynamics of faith, and in that way the broadening of the faith-question. Readers who are familiar with Richard Niebuhr's *The Meaning of Revelation* (1941) will easily recognize my indebtedness to him.

All this was put to the test in my first position as a theological teacher in Indonesia. The Indonesia years were an immersion in the complexities of intercultural communication and an introduction to a country saturated with religion, familiar with God and gods, in which Islam was omnipresent. Western theological questions with regard to secularization and revolution, and critical approaches to human faith turned out to be threatening for many. That challenged me to continue searching for a theological vision that could combine modern globalization with laborious interreligious and intercultural communication – or, in the vocabulary of those years: unite secularization and religion in the perspective of *Missio Dei*. Several Asian theologians – M.M. Thomas, Kosuke Koyama, Choan-Seng Song – presented themselves as helpful conversation partners.

Back in the Netherlands, after a brief interlude as a local pastor, a long period of teaching at the State University of Groningen committed me to the disciplines of missiology, ecumenics and Christian ethics. During those years, various forms of involvement with the World Council of Churches, particularly its Department of Faith and Order, proved inspiring. What caught my attention was a (sadly short-lived) study project, called 'The Unity of the Church and the Unity of Humankind'. It was started in the wake of the fourth assembly of the Council (1968) with its strong statement 'The church is bold in speaking of itself as the sign of the coming unity of mankind'. Although that boldness soon subsided in Faith and Order itself, the theological implications of the statement, more specifically in the interpretation of Ernst Lange, have occupied me ever since. The study-project could have helped Faith and Order to place reflection about church unity and theological consensus in a larger eschatological framework and to connect thinking about church and tradition with the (secular) problems of humankind – in other words, to take the priority of eschatology over ecclesiology seriously. The explicit choice of an 'ecclesiological focus' in the work of Faith and Order was, in my opinion, a mistake: it failed to do (theological) justice to the history and intentions of the ecumenical movement as a whole.

(The church focus – pervasively present in church and theology, and largely unquestioned – was and is responsible for the persistent second-rate position of the disciplines of ecumenics and missiology in the universe of academic theology. As long as the concerns for unity and mission are regarded as concerns and tasks of the church, secondary to its 'being', those disciplines will remain just appendices to the more 'substantial' work of systematic theology, instead of becoming part of it. As a consequence, 'world' remains an abstract reality, distinct from 'church', objectified as mission field rather than brought to consciousness as the context and breeding ground of tradition.)

The invasion of liberation theology in the 1980s was a major event (for me primarily in the work of Gustavo Gutiérrez and Jon Sobrino). Invasion, indeed: this theology intended to break into the prevailing academic-western theological discourse. Black theology, feminist theology, theology that chooses its starting point in the contexts of the then so-called 'third world' all agreed with liberation theology that meaningful 'God-talk' can only originate at the 'underside of history'. Concepts such as 'unity' are suspect because they tend to trivialize or even legitimize basically warped relations between races, classes, sexes, cultures and continents. 'Contextuality' became a key word. It problematized the idea of a 'Christian tradition' as a context-transcending, given reality. Contextual theology exposed the extent to which conflicts that afflict humankind are reflected in relations between Christian communities and in theological discourse, and thus in the tradition itself. In that way, humankind became a theological theme.

But contextual theology also drew attention to the crucial importance of culture(s) in the shaping of the Christian tradition. Culture – no longer understood as a stable coherence of ethnic and social characteristics, but as a permanent battle for identity and meaning – is the medium in which traditions take shape; the dynamics of memory and anticipation (history) expresses itself within the living world of cultural diversity. In that perspective, Robert Schreiter helped me to see that the Christian tradition is a 'series of local constructions of theology', which implies that the identity of the Christian faith is a never-ending experiment that takes place in the midst of the ongoing history of humankind. That ongoing history is itself an arena of systems of imagination, in which intercultural clashes and frontier-crossings play decisive roles, and in which plurality is never innocent.

How does humankind become a theological theme? Liberation theology would suggest that the conflicts of world society, in connection with the thrust of the Christ-event, should convert all theology to a consistent position of combat and resistance. The term reconciliation is suspect in this context, as it can be used to legitimize unjust and oppressive relations. However, it can also be understood to refer to a vision of humankind beyond oppression, liberation and conflict. That is the eschatological perspective the Christian tradition offers. To be sure, 'reconciliation' can be used (and it has very often been used) as cheap comfort that trivializes the struggles of humankind and the burdens of the human condition. But as we learn to see that the core insights of the Christian tradition are at stake precisely in 'worldly' conflicts, the perspective of reconciliation can also become a powerful incentive to take position. That is faith.

In other words, the world-question leads back to the faith-question. What is faith? It is not enough to define it in terms of the passive acceptance of 'truths', of a particular world view, or of personal attachment to a saviour figure, even though all those aspects can play a role. Faith is above all the adventure to live one's life in an overall perspective, to place the perennial interaction of self and world under the guidance of an imagination that is full of promise – a promise that touches not only the self but includes all, because the self is essentially linked to humankind and nature. The powerful Christian image of reconciliation presents itself both on the individual level and on the level of the human community as a whole. It opens the eyes of faith to see the depths of guilt in the human self and in human society, and it deeply problematizes the notion of autonomy. In other words, faith is a moral and existential choice of position.

Meanwhile, involvement in an international study project called 'Missiology and Western Culture' confronted me with philosophical developments that made it necessary to rethink the nature of the 'truth claim' of Christian faith. The modern-western consensus with regard to knowledge, truth and reality is crumbling. The idea that there is an indubitable foundation for knowledge is abandoned. Truth claims are dubious by definition; human interaction with reality is conditioned by contingent and changing language games; the demarcation between truth and imagination becomes fluid; the authority of 'grand narratives' is no longer valid; the trusted 'modern' scheme of subject and object, self and world, no longer holds.

The relation between self and reality and between rationality and imagination is more complex than one is inclined to think, and that, obviously, has an impact on the faith-question. The human self constructs a 'world' with the aid of images, metaphors and narratives. The self itself, long considered to be the unassailable starting point of individuality, turns out to be a by-product of individual and collective imaginations. Faith is attachment to a specific religious imagination that holds self, God and world together, and in doing so inspires and motivates.

A post-realist focus on the crucial role of (religious) imagination seemed to me to be able to address many of the concerns that I had accumulated over the years. In a post-realist approach, 'God' and 'world' are no longer seen as parts or aspects of an objectively existing universe that 'is there' over against an equally independent 'self'. It abandons the either/or realism of modernity, according to which human reason decides what is true or false. Above all, it delivers us from the pervasive dualism that has characterized the Christian tradition from its beginning: the tendency to hold on to a basic duality of God and world, church and world, revelation and reason, history and eschatology.

In premodern thinking, that duality was unproblematic, because it belonged to a world view in which everything was interconnected in a God-centred universe. In modern times, it became a problem, as the human self was enthroned as the judge of what ultimately counts as acceptable. All speech about God and revelation is then pushed to the defensive because it is taken out of the self-evident self-God-world coherence characteristic of premodernity. In that atmosphere of defensiveness, theological liberalism and confessional orthodoxy arose as two opposing theological trajectories. My hope is that a post-realist approach will ultimately create a synthesis between the two.

The various lines in my theological existence have resulted in a challenge to make a case for the Christian tradition that does justice both to its impressive history and to the context in which that history moves forward. I have presented the Christian faith as (never-ending) prayer: as a pattern of life in which dependence and hope are held together, and as a discipline not to lose sight of how much humankind is in need of reconciliation.

The paradigm of sacrifice remains the hard core of the faith. Ultimately, it is that core that makes the Christian faith difficult to embrace and to appropriate, regardless of age and context. Numerous efforts have been made to relativize or mitigate the paradigm, or to escape from it altogether. Those who take it seriously condemn themselves almost by definition to a minority position in the world. Nevertheless: it is of inestimable value that there will always be selves and communities that dedicate themselves to it – in a personal lifestyle, in various forms of community life, and in social and political initiatives that testify to hope for humankind.

Tjamsweer/Rasquert, Summer 2021

Index

afterlife, 80, 106-107
agnostic(ism), 36, 37, 43
anticipation, 21-23, 30, 31, 97-107 *and passim*
atheism, 1, 12, 61, 62, 65
autonomy, *vid* self
axis-age, 25, 27, 30

bricolage, 28-30

Christianity, 111-115 *and passim*
    in relation to other religions, 31, 85, 96, 102, 120, 121
cognitive (strategy, instrument), 4, 14, 41
commemoration, 22, 23, 29, 85, 88-96, 103, 104, 106, 110
conquest, spirituality of, 48, 49, 108, 119
cosmos, 78-80
creation, 78, 80-82 *and passim*
    in relation to reconciliation and redemption, 66, 81, 83, 84

death, 102-107 *and passim*
    of God, 60-62
dialogue, dialogical, 10, 11, 17, 29, 30, 38, 45, 46, 50, 54, 63, 70, 83, 121, 122

ecumenical movement, 112-116
Enlightenment, 1, 25, 26, 48, 49
eschaton, 58, 84, 93, 94, 100
eschatonomy, 58, 84
eschatology, 109, 111, 116, 117, 122-124, 126
eucharist, 93-95, 113, 115-118

evil, 53, 57, 62, 72, 82, 97, 98, 100
evolution, 4, 7, 12-14, 17, 19, 29, 34, 72, 73, 76-79, 81, 82, 119

faith, 10, 16, 17, 45, 46, 125, 126 *and passim*
    and science, 14, 40-43, 73, 76-80
fides (quae/qua), 2, 3, 30, 40, 41, 44, 83, 87, 88, 90, 91, 94, 111, 116
finitude, 33, 35, 82, 103, 105, 106
fundamentalism, 28-30

God, 60-70 *and passim*
    existence (of God), 1, 13, 14, 36, 37, 62, 63
guilt, 52-57 *and passim*
    confession of guilt, 55-57, 66, 95, 96, 117
guilt and reconciliation
    basic perspective, 52-55
    relation to withdrawal of God, 65-66
    dynamic of history, 76
    relation to finitude and death, 103-104
    relation to mission, 110

history, 21, 22, 74, 75 *and passim*
humankind, unity of, *passim*
    introductory definition, 15-19
    relation to religious traditions, 25-26, 30-31
    relation to guilt, 55-56
    relation to redemption, 75-76
    relation to kingdom of God, 100-101

Index

imagination, 6-19 *and passim*
introspection, 33-36

Jesus Christ, 87-96
    incarnation, 90, 91
    resurrection, 91, 92
    second coming, 95, 96
judg(e, ment), 52, 54, 58, 66, 68, 74, 84, 89, 96, 99, 101, 102, 110

kingdom (of God), 58, 73, 74, 76, 97-102, 106, 110, 119

love, 51, 57-59, 63, 65, 74, 82-84, 88, 94, 102-107, 119

memory, 21, 22, 30, 31, 87-96
mission, 108-121
    missionary movement, 108-111
monotheis(m, tic), 69, 70

negative theology, 65, 66, 69

omnipresence, omnipresent, 18, 53, 55, 57, 61, 66, 84, 94, 95, 124

(post)modern(ity), 1, 2, 16, 20, 26-31, 53, 60, 61, 122
prayer, 32-43 *and passim*

rationality, 8-11 *and passim*
reconciliation, *vid* guilt and reconciliation
    in relation to redemption and creation, 66, 81, 83, 84
redemption, 75-76 *and passim*
    in relation to creation and reconciliation, 66, 81, 83, 84
religion, *passim*
    religious imagination, 11, 12 *and passim*
    religious traditions, 23-26 *and passim*
revelation, 17, 23, 36, 63, 64, 98, 102, 122, 123, 126, 127

sacrifice, 28, 53, 93-96, 100, 102, 104, 105
science, *vid* faith and science
scripture(s), 40, 89, 90
secular(ization), 11, 24, 26-28, 30, 31, 37, 39, 41-44, 84, 98, 100, 122, 124
secularized, 2, 12, 39, 74, 118
self, 47-59 *and passim*
    self-God-world triad, 33, 34, 37, 38, 45, 64, 83, 84, 107
sin, 54-56, 93
subject, 48-50 *and passim*

theism, 61, 62, 72
theology, 41-43 *and passim*
tradition, 20-31 *and passim*
Trinity, 68-70

wager, 35, 37, 40, 46, 82, 120
world, 71-82, 119-121 *and passim*